PREACHING DURING A REVOLUTION

Patterns of Procedure

by

G. Ray Jordan

THE WARNER PRESS, ANDERSON, INDIANA

TO
THOSE STUDENTS
WHOSE COMMITMENT TO THE CHRIST
PRESENTS A CHALLENGE
TO MY OWN PREACHING
DURING A REVOLUTION

OTHER BOOKS BY

G. Ray Jordan

Religion That Is Eternal
Prayer That Prevails
Beyond Despair
You Can Preach!
The Emerging Revival
The Hour Has Come
The Supreme Possession
We Believe: A Creed That Sings
Look at the Stars!
Adventures in Radiant Living
We Face Calvary—and Life!
Why the Cross?
Faith That Propels
Courage That Propels
Intimate Interests of Youth
The Intolerance of Christianity
What Is Yours?

PREFACE

We are called to preach today during a revolution. This setting and this challenge are emphasized in the pages that follow, as· I discuss various critical conditions. It is my desire, to be sure, to present facts which are relevant under any circumstances for those concerned with the message of Christianity. But these truths become even more vital in a time of social and international upheaval.

In addition to these contemporary crises, we must also deal with a revolution in techniques and methods posed by the skills of mass communication. As we communicate, we find ourselves grappling with terms that keep calling our attention to the fact that these are days of revolution. Consider these: iron curtain, inter-continental missiles, nuclear warfare, fallout shelters, bomb shelters, astro-jets, earth satellites.

Preaching has been seriously affected by the universal upheaval, of which these terms speak. Although the basic principles of homiletics remain, many emphases and techniques have changed. It is my desire, therefore, not merely to define sharply and present plainly effective patterns of preaching, but to discuss each separately, so that it will be quite clear.

Many sermons, of course, contain various patterns. For instance, the introduction may present a life situation approach, or it may depict information with inspiration. In the same sermon the body of the message may be thematic or expository. So, the conclusion may be only a brief summary, or affirmation with reason. Thus it will illustrate "theology that thrills." This possible variety is evident to the earnest student of the art of preaching.

Eager to pinpoint every principle presented, I have attempted to demonstrate each blueprint from actual sermons, instead of simply commending it. This is another indication of the pragmatic nature of the book.

An example of this practical pattern of procedure is emphasized in the chapter, "The Counselor in the Pulpit." Any individual who presents the Christian message effectively today must know the basic procedures of psychotherapy. Only to the degree that our hearers feel we understand them personally, will they trust us to explain the practical emphases of the gospel as sources of strength.

It is, of course, my earnest hope that readers will quickly see that the themes presented deal with principles of preaching which are timeless. But in a more important sense, it is my desire to point out specific ways in which any writer of sermons can execute his own plans and make meaningful the logic of his own outlines and illustrations of biblical truth. If, therefore, numbers of us, whose profession gives us unusual opportunity to become creative writers, can more quickly and easily grasp these fundamental principles and basic rules, I shall count myself fortunate.

My deep gratitude goes to Dean William R. Cannon for making possible special study in the preparation of this book.

—G.R.J.

CONTENTS

I

PREACHING DURING A REVOLUTION

If we are going to preach at all, it will be during a revolution. Everywhere in our world there are rebellions, insurrections, debacles, political revolts, and catastrophic changes.

People in every area of life are feeling the force of this world revolution. Although, so far, we in America have apparently been able to avoid most of its sweeping economic influence, actually our total life is being seriously affected by what is going on elsewhere in the world. The social and political earthquakes are so violent we do not need a seismograph to record them!

I. A Dangerous Day

Every alert and dedicated minister knows that this is a difficult day in which to preach. Far from being debatable, this statement is now almost a trite truism. The longer we are engaged in this profession, the more keenly we feel the tensions of our day. Many sense danger as well as difficulty.

Recall the death, a few years ago, of a man under whose control lived eight hundred million people. At his funeral not one word was spoken concerning immortality, the meaning of life, hope for tomorrow, or the worth of man. There are now approximately one billion people caught in the meshes of the philosophy Stalin represented, although he himself has been removed from his pedestal of honor. Far more than this number are swayed by ideas and ideals which are not Christian.

Consider the desperate urgency of these facts. They come with extra force to some of us when we recall those

9

twenty-one thousand young men and women studying at the University of Moscow. One day a cold chill came over a few of us during a visit to that institution. This chill was not caused by the rain falling at the moment. Rather, it was a chill of the soul, for we were informed by authorities, who spoke with pride, that only exact sciences, with no religious interpretation or assumption, were taught at this place. Indeed, if a student believes in God, he loses his scholarship.

Since, moreover, the Soviets consider the humanities of so much less importance, instruction in them has been confined to the old buildings in the center of the city. The finest and best, the most modern equipment Russia has, is given entirely to the advancement and study of science. Even the value of the scholarships in the area of the humanities is much less than that of those offered to the students in the sciences.

Further cause for deep thought was provided us, as representatives of democratic America, when we learned that university professors are among the highest salaried people in Russia. Indeed, the Soviet teachers do not merely receive excellent pay; they have comfortable working conditions and are highly respected in their communities. Furthermore, every young man or woman who earnestly desires an education is given one at the expense of the government. The individual has only to maintain the required scholastic standard and remain committed to the philosophy of Marx and Lenin, as adjusted to contemporary communism. Here is a revolution no one can escape!

Then there are those radical changes relevant to our security, brought about by the development of the atom and hydrogen bombs. All who understand science and military procedures clearly see that no civilization can survive a third world war conducted with the techniques for destruction now available.

Two discussions in an old theological book succinctly summarize our situation. The first chapter in that volume was titled "Hell." Chapter two was captioned "Hell Continued." This is precisely the situation as we face it. We have had an armistice but no peace. Each day we hope that we may avoid complete collapse. But we know that there is always the possibility of a few people becoming insane enough to touch off the "powder keg" that could destroy us.

The fact that it is a difficult day in which to preach—and to live—searches our minds and pains our hearts. Many, indeed, feel that ours has become a day of despair.

II. OUR ATTITUDE

What will the preacher do under these circumstances? He can, of course, throw up his hands and surrender to defeatism. He can tell people that the "day of the Lord" is at hand and mean that doom is our certain destiny. He may become so downcast that he will sing a song of sorrow. He may even refuse to express himself with any music! Often he will be tempted to become a cynic.

If, however, we are going to deliver an effective Christian message, we cannot yield to any of these temptations. We cannot even raise the nostalgic question suggested centuries ago by the captives who refused to lift their voices in happy song by the waters of Babylon: "How shall we sing the Lord's song in a strange land?" (Ps. 137:4). Rather we will realize that *a crisis is an opportunity.*

Indeed, if we make any lasting contribution to the welfare of man, we shall have to understand that, at the moment, the one place where we need to sing is "by the waters of Babylon"! Contemporary crises demand courage. If we fail our people now, we help destroy their confidence in the gospel itself. Soon we shall have no message of hope.

Obviously we dare not adopt the emotional reaction of Schopenhauer who wailed, "Our condition is so wretched that utter annihilation would be preferable." He declared that there was nothing anyone could do about the situation.

11

He insisted that God is powerless to prevent evil, or he has no desire to abolish it, or there is no God who can do anything. In like manner a popular contemporary novelist, probably representing hosts of people, says he cannot understand why God created man anyway. Many of us agree with J. B. Phillips when he says, "Our society bears all the marks of a God-starved community."[1]

Fortunately, throughout all history many have faced crises and refused to capitulate to despair. Centuries ago when Isaiah went into the Temple to worship, he was pained by conditions which seemed certain to make him despair. His great leader and hero was dead. Uzziah had ruled for fifty-two years. For young Isaiah, this king was the incarnation of power, ability, and greatness. With the exception of one blot on his reign, his kingship was of a high order. Now he was gone. The hopes of the young man fell to the ground. Despondency laid hold on him. He was sure that the lights were going out. He could almost hear the "tramp, tramp, tramp," of the troops gathering to attack Judah.

Depressed with a sense of defeatism, he went into the Temple to pour out his feelings. Instead, however, of continuing his search for a wailing wall, he caught a vision. He glimpsed the majesty of Jehovah. He saw another throne high and lifted up, and on it a King the like of whose glory no earthly ruler had known. Then he began to understand. Uzziah, who had been the incarnation of power for Isaiah was dead, but Power still lived. Uzziah, who had been the embodiment of worthy, regal splendor, had gone, but heavenly glory still shone on. The king of Judah was dead, but the King of kings was still on his throne wielding his divine scepter triumphantly.

It is this kind of experience which must come to us if we are to have a message of hope in a day of difficulty. Indeed, it seems to be painfully obvious that there will

---

[1] *God Our Contemporary* (Macmillan, New York, 1960), p. viii.

never be another time of ease and mental relaxation such as our grandfathers and great-grandfathers enjoyed. It seems clear that the tranquillity which belonged to the mid-Victorian era will never return to our world. This, however, is all the more reason why we must find peace in the midst of tension, power where only weakness seems evident, purpose where there seems to be no plan for mankind.

III. WHAT TO PREACH

Always vital, the content of the sermons we offer our hearers in a day like this has become more important than ever before. Always a *sine qua non* of virile preaching, Christian theology is now more than ever an indispensable requisite for effective sermons. These crises remind us that three great themes have constantly challenged the keenest thinkers: (1) Does man have worth? (2) Does the world have meaning? (3) Is there a God capable of substantiating a positive answer to each of these questions? We who preach must find plan, purpose, and power for life.

In spite of Marxism and secularism, multitudes long for a realization of God. Many want the unknown God to portray himself in such a dramatic way that they can be confident of his reality. Some cry out that they are dying, that they are all alone. For such it is increasingly clear that the Christian faith is no longer optional; it is a requisite for life.

The author of Hebrews 11:1 keenly felt this when he tried to define faith. He not merely expressed his own feelings but clearly indicated the direction in which we, too, must move if we are to have any hope of meeting life happily and confidently. Recall some of the familiar translations of the original statement:

1. Now faith is the substance of things hoped for, the evidence of things not seen (KJV).
2. Now faith means we are confident of what we hope for, convinced of what we do not see (Moffatt).

3. Now faith is a confident assurance of that for which we hope, a conviction of the reality of things which we do not see (Weymouth).

4. Now faith is the assurance of things hoped for, the conviction of things not seen (RSV).

5. Faith means putting our full confidence in the things we hope for; it means being certain of things that we cannot see (Phillips).

6. Faith gives substance to our hopes, and makes us certain of realities we do not see (NEB).

This kind of confidence does not come easily. It is not wrapped in a package and made available over some counter. It is not left on our doorsteps like a bottle of milk for which we rush out in the early morning before we are hardly awake. Nor does faith come by opening our mouths and shutting our eyes. We do not swallow it as a pill is taken—just gulped down. Christian trust is terrifically expensive. In fairness we have to let our people know that. Mr. Lewisham, a fictional character, called on God for faith in the silence of the night. It was to be made available immediately if Mr. Lewisham's patronage was valued! Nevertheless, it was not so delivered! It never will be.

Again, we have to remind our people that this faith does not remove disappointments. They are inevitable in a world like ours. Christian assurance, however, does brace us for difficulties. It makes it possible for us to stand up to life. It brings mental poise, steady nerves. It was because of his belief in God that Paul gained an almost uncanny sense of confidence. Hear him as he writes: "I am suffering all this because I am a preacher, an apostle and teacher: yet I am not ashamed; for I know him whom I have believed, and I am persuaded that he is able to guard that which I have committed unto him against that day" (II Tim. 1:12).

This faith makes possible true reverence for life—again brought vividly to our attention by Albert Schweitzer, as

14

well as by others who insist that the dignity of man is intrinsically involved in our relationship to God.

Indeed, only a great theology is adequate for any of us. The question, Is there a God who really cares for us? is no longer merely academic. In some way we face it every day. Is God able to do what needs to be done? World conditions force this issue on us. A deity worthy of worship is no mental luxury. Such is a necessity for anyone who would have any lasting peace of mind.

Ours is a difficult day in which to preach Christian ethics. At the same time, the crisis is one which demands nothing less than the basic moral principles proclaimed by Jesus. It underscores—with red ink—the world family idea Christ insisted upon when he directed us to pray, *"Our Father . . ."* This sense of interrelatedness is the only realism which is dependable for our world.

The idea of immortality, too, comes to us with new force. But the wise preacher will not glibly assure people that there is a future for them, and therefore they can indulge in the comfort of thinking that everyone will be cared for tomorrow. Rather, we should make our parishioners, as well as ourselves, uncomfortable about anticipating a future in which we shall have to keep remembering that *we left a world in hell and did nothing to make it less hellish.* At the same time, the Christian preacher with a keen mind and a great heart proclaims a gospel that promises power for the present and confidence for tomorrow.

The revolution is here. Long ago millions of us should have been concerned with a new world. Now there must be, not merely a new world, but one good world that lives up to the highest moral and ethical standards possible—or there will be no world at all! We have to go far beyond those who deny or ignore the reality of the Deity. We must insist that as Christians we *now* give God a chance to build a better world.

IV. How to Preach

The minister who has a message for this dangerous and difficult day must also learn the art of delivering his message. One of the major skills a preacher must learn is to utilize specific patterns of procedure in the most practical ways possible. Each sermon blueprint is important. Furthermore, there are key words which quickly suggest the only way in which we dare to preach today. They serve as signposts indicating the direction in which we must move.

In the first place, we must preach *understandingly*. This means that we are not merely to grasp the message ourselves but also to establish mental rapport with our congregation. We can cultivate this ability by reading, by meditating, and by observing the experiences of other people. *The Diary of a Young Girl*, the story of a teen-age Jewish girl who lost her life just prior to the close of World War II, suggests how this may be done. Anne Frank was hiding in a building in Amsterdam, along with members of her family and some of their friends.

In deeply moving simplicity her diary discloses the mind and heart of this young girl. She bares her secret thoughts, her philosophy, her attitudes toward people, the world, and tragedy. The way in which the pages of her diary, scattered on the floor of the building by the Nazis, were found by one who recognized their worth, is itself exciting.

Reading books of this kind, we can begin to understand and enter into the suffering and trials of other people. Manifestly, any minister who is not pained when he recalls the millions who were thrust into gas chambers a few years ago can hardly understand those of his own flock whose sufferings are too great for verbal expression.

It is possible, also, to appreciate the experiences of our fellows by observation. We witness the affliction and misery of others until we feel with them. Manifestly we can really understand people only as we think of their needs and respond to them. The person who, in hours of imaginative meditation, has knelt with Christ in Gethsemane and walked with him to Calvary will increasingly be able to appreciate the phrase "redemptive worry." We know we cannot speak effectively to those who suffer if we present truth in a take-it-or-leave-it fashion. Neither Gethsemane nor Golgotha suggests unconcern or animallike contentment. Certainly we should learn to use our own disappointments in establishing mental rapport with the perplexed. Our attitudes should demonstrate that we grasp at least something of the meaning of the Cross.

Again, as Christian ministers, we will speak *earnestly*. Evangelistic preaching is only one example of the necessity of our proclaiming the good news zealously. This adverb is relevant to every kind of sermon, every gospel message. Whatever may be our specific personal method of delivering sermons, our attitude must always demonstrate earnestness. Many feel the most satisfactory way to present our message is by means of a conversational tone with the tempo properly stepped up to meet the needs of the congregation. Certainly this method can be characterized by genuine concern.

As a matter of fact, the kind of material we use can itself speak loudly enough for all our congregation to hear. Ponder the declaration of Prime Minister Nehru that we must have a "passion for peace." With reference to this, he informed some of us who were interviewing him that practically all the nuclear power India has is being channeled into peaceful uses. Whatever our reaction to Nehru's professed desire for friendship among all nations and races, obviously international understanding is a requisite for world peace.

In the area of family relationship, the story of *Karen*[2] presents the necessity of earnestness as few contemporary books do. Karen's parents planned and dreamed for her, anticipating a happy future for their child. But Karen

---

[2]*Karen*, by Marie Killilea (Prentice-Hall, Englewood Cliffs, N.J.)

weighed less than two pounds when she was born. After time spent in an incubator, Karen was strong enough to be brought home. Not long after, her parents became aware that something was wrong. Pronounced cerebral palsy necessitated their seeing physician after physician. Nineteen specialists offered no hope. One told them to go home and take out all the insurance they could, since the child might live many years and they should protect themselves economically.

In spite of numerous discouragements, the father and mother kept spending time, money, energy, and love until they received help. Thus, Karen developed until she could walk, talk, feed herself—and tests revealed an IQ far above the average child of her age.

Deep desire must characterize the preacher who would deliver the gospel message effectively. The interest of people in what we say will necessarily be conditioned by our own expression of concern. It is not reasonable to anticipate that the tide of enthusiasm in any service will rise higher than it does in the leader. We condition the congregation by our attitude and the spirit in which we discuss God's Word.

Also, we are to speak *intelligently*. Most of us realize that preaching is often ineffective essentially because it is not directed toward the wills and nobler emotions of our people. We must aim truth directly at the hearts of our hearers if we expect to bring them life. Apropos of this, Thomas Aquinas pointed out that God is "intelligible light." We are always to share this insight with our congregation. It was Paul who said, "I had rather speak five words with my understanding . . . than ten thousand words in an unknown tongue" (I Cor. 14:19).

So clear-cut should be the presentation of our sermons that the congregation will feel, "This is altogether reasonable." When the custodian has turned out the lights and the members of the congregation are on their way to their homes, in calm moments of serious thought they should always be able to feel that what we have said is dependable. This is doubly important when we are in the midst of a revolution and so many irresponsible speakers are clamoring to be heard.

Certainly the effective minister speaks *challengingly*. Succinctly and plainly Jesus illustrated this idea when he said, "If any man will come after me, let him . . . take up his cross and follow me" (Matt. 16:24). This attitude and spirit must characterize the message of the minister who anticipates a fortunate response on the part of his hearers.

Consider an ex-soldier, formerly a paratrooper. Now the minister of a church of less than a hundred members, seeking to be guided by this principle of divine daring, he constantly appeals to his hearers to give all that they have and are to Christ. No one who applies for membership is permitted to unite with the church until he has had a year in which to prove the genuineness of his interest and the reality of his concern. The members regularly study to show themselves approved unto God and diligently seek to learn, as students, the truth of their religion.

Recall also how Phillips Brooks lured his hearers to new heights. He dared them to accept the divine power, so they could move up to a level on which they had never previously lived. A retired Harvard professor recently told Theodore Parker Ferris, "As I look back upon it, the thing that stands out pre-eminently is the elevation which he [Brooks] sustained, and to which he constantly drew us."[3] No wonder scores of students made their way to Trinity Church every Sunday! They heard a man who challenged them to move up to a higher life than they had ever known.

True Christian ministers will not merely dare people to be *better;* they will challenge them to be *Christlike.* To be sure, this places a heavy responsibility on those of us who speak for God, since only as we ourselves demon-

---

[3]Quoted in *When I Became a Man* (Oxford University Press, New York, 1957), p. 178.

strate the reality of the religion we proclaim is it reasonable to anticipate an eager response. Such a responsibility, however, is itself part of the challenge of the Cross.

Reality in religion is manifested in very practical ways—sometimes altogether unexpected. Consider Elizabeth Pilenko of whom Victor Gollancz reminds us. A Russian living in Paris, she took the place of a Jewish girl who was to be sent to the incinerators. Elizabeth was burned in her stead. Even if her action had never been known, rightly reasons Gollancz; if, in fact, no one had ever witnessed it, and if the Jewish girl herself had lost her life immediately afterwards, Elizabeth was doing "the only thing that can answer the world's evil."[4] Indeed, her action does live, and the world is to some degree a better place because of it. She is a modern example of what it means to respond to the challenge of the cross.

V. When to Preach

To suggest that there is the possibility of our deciding when to preach seems an unfortunate kind of humor. We know that we have to preach each Sunday as well as during those other scheduled services which come with such regularity. Nevertheless, in our moments of truest spiritual discernment we are aware that we do not, indeed, we *cannot,* preach unless the atmosphere of the service makes preaching possible.

Frank Boreham, writing of using the same sermon at two different churches one Sunday, makes this truth painfully vivid. In one sanctuary the response was richly rewarding. Numbers of people made decisions for Christ. In the other church, no one seemed particularly interested. There was no evidence of concern, no visible response whatever. Yet, as far as he could tell, Mr. Boreham had presented the identical message with the same earnest appeal.

A number of years ago, I attended a service of worship

---

[4] *My Dear Timothy* (Simon and Schuster), p. 241.

at St. Martin-in-the-Fields, London, which underscored this necessity of rapport between people and preacher. Dr. H. R. L. Sheppard was preaching. The church was crowded. Although I arrived some time before the hour of the service, it was necessary to go to the balcony for a seat. "Dick" Sheppard did not preach what one might call a "great" sermon. His message was simple and plain, couched in language the humblest hearer could understand. The response, however, was notable. As I watched the congregation, as well as the preacher, I became increasingly aware of how eagerly the people listened. Not merely did they center their attention upon the minister; many of them leaned over in an effort to be nearer the pulpit, as though they were determined not to miss a word. They seemed to be saying, "Speak on, Dr. Sheppard; we are listening. We are offering our assistance. We are cooperating in every way we know how."

As the congregation prays, so we preach. There is no effective sermon unless the worshipers create an atmosphere in which the message is heard understandingly and appreciatively. The wise preacher will teach his laymen how to pray. Indeed, *we do not really preach until the congregation prays for us.* We may utter words, present an essay, deliver a discourse, but the effective gospel sermon is possible only to the degree that the hearers create conditions which give it meaning and force.

VI. WHERE TO PREACH

When we ask, "Where shall we preach?" again the question seems superficial and the answer altogether obvious. A church has been assigned to us and we are responsible for the message being delivered in that particular pulpit. Actually, however, we preach effectively only from high spiritual levels of experience. Only so is our message heard in the valley of need and desire.

An experience of Handley Page, one of the best-known early English pilots, dramatically presents this truth. This

21

pioneer airman tells of a trip he was making in the first years of what has now become one of the great industries of the world. He relates a few facts concerning his landing at Kobar, India. After leaving this city, while winging his way to his next destination, he became aware of the presence of an extra passenger in his plane. The telltale sound of gnawing was evidence enough. Manifestly a rat had been attracted by the smell of food. But there was danger that the pitiless teeth would destroy some delicate part of the mechanism of the machine. For this early plane was a far cry from the modern ones so familiar to those who travel by air today.

What should Mr. Page do? He suddenly recalled that rats are made for low altitudes, not high ones. He pointed the nose of his plane at the sharpest angle he dared and kept soaring. Scarcely able to breathe, he listened but could hear no sound of gnawing teeth. He still kept his plane pointed toward the heavens! There were no pressurized cabins, and the danger he incurred was frightfully real. He kept flying at this altitude, however, until he was certain there was no noise suggesting the presence of his stowaway. When he finally brought his plane down at the next airfield, Mr. Page looked back in the cockpit. There he saw a dead rat.

The parable is vivid, but not too powerful in its implications. The preacher who is effective today must live so high spiritually that no deadly foe of bitterness, jealousy, or ill will—or any other enemy—will wreck his character and his profession.

From high levels the minister who represents Christ will speak appealingly for the sake of all mankind. This has always been true. But during the revolutionary days in which we are compelled to preach it is imperative if we have anything to say to which our parishioners will listen.

II

IMAGINATION: INDISPENSABLE TALENT

Imagination is one of the most misunderstood words in the English language. Too many people think it is a sign of immaturity. We anticipate children exercising this faculty. Sometimes we say, "They stretch their imaginations," thus suggesting elasticity of mind. Although we do not usually condemn the very young for being imaginative, we *do* expect them to outgrow this "tendency to exaggerate."

When, however, we use language like this, we indicate that we do not understand imagination. Indeed, to scorn this talent by refusing to cultivate it means that we deteriorate both mentally and spiritually.

For imagination is not merely the greatest moral lever known to man, as Wordsworth has said; it is also that insight by means of which we catch the meaning of words, the temperature of the spiritual atmosphere, the unexpressed attitudes of people. It enables us to see what others do not see. Often, by it we are able to make many of our comrades see what we see. Artists, painters, writers, speakers—all must exercise imagination if they rise above the ordinary. Instead of scientists being exceptions to the rule, they demonstrate it daily. By means of it they have learned much about nuclear power. Indeed, it is necessary for every profession.

Never has imagination been so vital for the Christian preacher as today. Without this quality we fail to under-. stand our world and descend to deadly dullness. It is no wonder that others besides John Masefield have felt that, although man's body is faulty and his mind untrustworthy, his imagination has made him remarkable. Certainly neither the preacher nor his message becomes extraordinary without it. It is a *sine qua non* of our profession.

During a revolution, however, the Christian use of imagination is more important than most of us can even begin to surmise. When there are so many writers and speakers talking about the "post-Christian" age, unless we understand what provokes this unexpected discussion, and at the same time gain new insights into the eternal truth of the teachings of Christ, we shall not have a relevant message. We shall not even be able to avoid meaningless clichés and worn-out phrases which no longer carry any truth vital for contemporary society.

I. Poetic Power for the Preacher

We readily understand that imagination is a requisite for the successful poet, but insight into lyrical beauty and rhythm is also vital for the preacher. Any minister who is lacking in this ability is seriously handicapped. Only when we understand the genius of the poet is it possible for us properly to evaluate the worth of imagination. Just, for instance, to the degree that we see beauty as Wordsworth did, can we either come under its spell or have it become a part of our very being and thus influence those to whom we speak.

> I wandered lonely as a cloud
> That floats on high o'er vales and hills,
> When all at once I saw a crowd,
> A host, of golden daffodils;
> Beside the lake, beneath the trees,
> Fluttering and dancing in the breeze.
>
> . . . .
>
> . . . Oft, when on my couch I lie,
> In vacant or in pensive mood,
> They flash upon that inward eye
> Which is the bliss of solitude;
> And then my heart with pleasure fills,
> And dances with the daffodils.[1]

---

[1] William Wordsworth, "I Wandered Lonely as a Cloud."

Ten thousand times ten thousand people had seen daffodils long before Wordsworth wrote these lines, but no one can see daffodils after reading these lines understandingly without appreciating beauty as never before. He comes to see the vital relationship of loveliness to all life.

Wordsworth possessed this remarkable quality in an extraordinary way. It is one of the secrets of his power as a poet.

> My heart leaps up when I behold
> A rainbow in the sky;
> So was it when my life began;
> So is it now I am a man;
> So be it when I shall grow old,
> Or let me die![2]

Indeed, we are already dead if our hearts do not leap up when we behold a rainbow in the sky! It may be we are not yet buried, and our family has not paid the mortician, but mentally and spiritually in the area of beauty we are without life. In a pronounced sense this is true of the preacher. He must possess the poet's sensitivity to beauty—not merely of the physical world but also of that inherent in the human spirit.

We can never make our congregation come to life unless we ourselves have a contagious resilience of spirit. It was written of Stevenson that he died with a thousand stories in his heart. The minister must live with a thousand stories in his mind and heart—stories of other people's daily experiences carefully kept and wisely understood. They are a spiritual asset that no one of us can ever overestimate.

II. The Creative Power of Imagination

Actually imagination has always been one of the greatest creative forces in life. In every area we see this truth underscored. Could there have been a more dramatic or in-

---

[2] Wordsworth, "My Heart Leaps Up When I Behold."

disputably accurate manifestation of its power than the experience of two men from Dayton, Ohio, on the sand dunes of North Carolina, a little more than fifty years ago? They had the idea that they could fly a heavier-than-air machine. Newspapermen laughed at them. Cartoonists drew what they thought were funny pictures, depicting this "silly idea." But two men had imagination! Whether it was the result of observing a dragonfly, or whether there was some other explanation for the idea that these men had of keeping a heavier-than-air machine in the air, is of little consequence. They saw clearly something which most people did not see—or believe possible.

December 17, 1903, was a notable day. Historians will treasure the record. Orville Wright kept a heavier-than-air machine in the air twelve seconds. Later that same day his brother Wilbur kept this same machine in the air for fifty-nine seconds, flying 852 feet. Nothing will ever be the same again. Nothing *can* ever be the same. It was like waving a magician's wand. Transportation had a new birth. The world became a neighborhood that day. Wars can never be fought again as before. Problems never before imagined are now involved in all national and international relationships. People can never be the same, for life is different. *All history took a turn on that notable day!* Two men created what their imaginations had seen. They gave the world something which had not been real, but which became quite real.

Similarly, in the area of science imagination has enabled trained men to discover that within an iron bar are millions of molecules made up of atoms, and within the atom many electrons. Thus, too, any student of astronomy may see the stars, but imagination makes it possible to see the whirling worlds of the universe. By means of telescopes almost anybody can learn to study heavenly bodies he cannot see with the naked eye, but eyes of the soul are necessary if he sees purpose in the heavenly bodies he studies.

Hence, scientists with insight do not smile incredulously at new and unexplored possibilities. Caesar would have laughed if a radio or television set had been described to him. The thought of his words, *"Veni, vidi, vici,"* reaching the ears of millions of unseen hearers would have seemed only the dream of a distorted mind. Milton's *Paradise Lost* was not written with a fountain pen. The first draft of Dante's *Divine Comedy* was not typed on a Royal or an Underwood. These are only a few "impossibles" which have become realities because of men's imagination.

III. Effective Speakers Use Imagination

In certain areas men have always known how to use this talent of imagination. Standing by the pyramids near Cairo, Napoleon demonstrated the reason for his tremendous sway over the minds of men when he said, "Soldiers, forty centuries look down on you!" He was quite accurate in declaring that "imagination rules the world."

The most effective ministers have known the power of imagination and have demonstrated it with remarkable finesse. George Whitefield often manifested the force of this asset. On a certain occasion the faultlessly correct Lord Chesterfield listened to Whitefield preach. The great evangelist, who knew how to use words with moving power, was describing a blind beggar led by a little dog. A fragile string, he told his hearers, was tied around the neck of the dog. The other end of the string was in the left hand of the beggar. In his right hand the beggar carried a cane with which he tapped his way along the walk. Whitefield told how the fragile string broke, how the dog ran off, and how the blind pedestrian continued groping his way with his cane. Dramatically he described the man stumbling along toward a precipice. Suddenly the cane dangled in the air and slipped from the grasp of the blind beggar into the abyss below. The man slowly groped forward, reaching for the cane. Unwittingly he was hovering over the brink of the chasm. The tension was more than even the cynical

Chesterfield could stand. Leaping to his feet, he shouted, "By heaven, he's gone!"

Few of us are as able as Whitefield to make our hearers see so vividly. Nevertheless, we know that without some degree of that ability we shall not move men. Hence the need for appreciating and cultivating our imaginations, particularly today.

Compelled to compete with radio and television, we are driven to the realization that imagination is a requisite of effective preaching. Television may push thousands of preachers out of their pulpits; for the producers of its vivid personalities and incidents know well the value of imagination. Any speaker who is not capable of making others see what they have never seen and feel what they may never have felt concerning the issues of life is doomed to failure. Such a person may soon find himself in the position of the man who had lost his pulpit. When another applied for the vacancy, he was told, "The Rev. Mr. Jones did not leave a vacancy." Certainly the minister who does not cultivate the talent of imagination will scarcely be missed when he does move.

Indeed, without this spiritual asset any speaker becomes increasingly uninteresting. The gospel, however, is vital to every phase of life; it is vivid, dramatic, appealing, intriguing. It is more than these. When it is presented in a way worthy of its character, it always provokes keen interest and often, excitement.

IV. Sermons Must Demonstrate Imagination

Fortunately there are sermons which demonstrate the value of imagination. The preacher who helps to change the thinking of people and who convinces their minds of the dependability and worth of Christ's message and way of life must possess far more than ordinary talent or insight. He must have the ability to make his indifferent and unconcerned hearers see themselves as they were when first they declared their loving loyalty to Christ, and also what they hoped they would be after ten, twenty, forty years following that momentous hour of their decision.

1. OUR BEST SELF

If he is able to get them to contrast their best selves with what they now are, he is on the highway that leads to effective preaching. Only the speaker with the power of imagination can ever make others willing to see themselves as they are. Such a person, however, will use every fair and honorable technique to make the members of his congregation open their spiritual eyes.

> Across the fields of long ago
> There often comes to me
> A little lad with face aglow—
> The boy I used to be.
>
> He watches, listens, takes my hand,
> And walks awhile with me,
> Then he asks me if I've made myself
> The man I planned to be.

The effective evangelistic preacher will make us see not merely our worst selves but also our potentially better selves—the selves we may be as the result of accepting divine grace. He may use an incident like that which occurred in a Pullman car when the train was bringing people home from a nationally known horse race. The writer who relates this incident found himself in the same Pullman car with numbers of men who had lost heavily by betting on the wrong horses. They were drinking and swearing about their "bad luck."

Near the front of the car was a little boy of preschool age, his mother having entrusted him to the care of the Pullman porter. The porter had made down the lower berth. As the train rattled along the tracks at seventy miles an hour, the little boy knelt by the side of his berth and began to pray in his high treble voice. Everybody in the car became quiet. Men who had been raucous and loud in their profane references to their "luck" listened in a kind of subdued awe. Finishing his prayer, the lad concluded with "amen," and crawled into the lower berth. One man, the loudest and most profane, exclaimed, "My God! What is it I have lost that this child has!"

By using techniques which stimulate imagination the wise preacher cultivates the ability to make many of his hearers see that although they may have lost something grand and great, *by the power of God it can be restored.* So we work daily to increase our capacity to make our hearers see and feel the dynamic power of truth. All the while we know that our ability to increase the insight of our hearers will be contingent, to a marked degree, upon the power of our own imagination.

Indeed, we are forced to agree with many psychiatrists that the mark of a healthy mind is in the ability to simplify the expression of an idea. Certainly, aloofness of attitude or of verbal expression is not for the preacher who desires to be heard and understood. Hear Tennyson:

> *Break, break, break,*
> *On thy cold gray stones, O Sea!*
> *And I would that my tongue could utter*
> *The thoughts that arise in me.*
>
> . . . .
>
> *And the stately ships go on*
> *To their haven under the hill;*
> *But O for the touch of a vanish'd hand,*
> *And the sound of a voice that is still!*
>
> *Break, break, break,*
> *At the foot of thy crags, O Sea!*
> *But the tender grace of a day that is dead*
> *Will never come back to me.*[3]

---

[3]Alfred Lord Tennyson, "Break, Break, Break."

Or consider this verbal expression of a vivid imagination —and do not call it humanizing God. It is far too meaningful for that. Just recall December. We are in the Advent season and we read: "God walked down the stairs with a baby in His arms." That does it!

2. EYES THAT SEE

We can at least partially understand what Helen Keller had in mind when a thoughtless child looked into her face and asked "Isn't it awful not to have two good eyes?" Knowing that Miss Keller was quite mature, Miss Sullivan relayed the question with her fingers. Without a moment's hesitation, speaking with her fingers and with the help of Miss Sullivan, Miss Keller answered, "Not half so bad as having two good eyes and not being able to see." She is right! Only as we grasp truth are we able to make others see and feel its power.

Of the many themes which necessitate insight and understanding, that of the family takes high rank. It is not merely a theme or a topic. It suggests the most intricate human relationships, involving society, sex, romance, love. If we cannot see into the minds and hearts of our people, we cannot help them. Indeed, we may discover that we have not even spoken to them. A mere recital of facts and figures, a deadly dull exhortation to preserve and protect the family, is altogether futile.

We know that in America the tide is moving too rapidly in the direction of domestic disintegration. We are also aware that no civilization has ever been able to survive the loss of its home life. Realizing this fact, however, does not guarantee our doing anything about it. Actually, any hope for our homes is contingent on our cultivating attitudes of understanding and of appreciative response on the part of each member of the family.

This is possible only as we are willing to put ourselves in each other's place. An Old Testament writer stated the principle this way: "I sat where they sat" (Ezek. 3:15). The modern psychologist declares that we must be willing "to walk in the shoes" of the other person. Certainly we are never truly Christian in our homes until we have the ability to crawl into the skins of other people. Only so do we understand them, sense their sorrows, and feel their agony of body and mind.

Thus when Jesus said we were to do unto others as we would have them do unto us, in one succinct sentence he emphasized the necessity of imagination, without which we dare not try to do to others as we would have them do to us. Actually, we harm other people when we attempt to live by the Golden Rule unless we understand them, appreciate their thoughts, and enter helpfully into the perplexed confusion of their minds and hearts. We must project ourselves into their places. This demands insight of the keenest and most spiritual quality.

Some sociologists tell us that the lines of neither race nor sex can really be crossed. If that is true, it serves to underscore the tremendous importance of cultivating the ability of understanding other people by projecting ourselves into their places.

3. MALICIOUS GOSSIP

Pointing out the terror of wrecking character with words requires even more care and finesse in the art of awaking imagination. At some time or other each of us needs to feel the pain malicious gossip may cause. A story widely circulated by the English writer Ronald Selby Wright may help us awaken dull minds. A salesman in Cairo, Egypt, showed Dr. Wright a rather large signet ring, the kind a man might wear. As the salesman pressed on a little catch in the side, the ring opened, showing a hollow cavity in the middle of it. "It is," explained the owner of the shop, "a poison ring. You see," he said, "you put the poison in there. Then you close the ring, and when you press—so— you can drop the poison into somebody's cup and no one knows." It was an interesting idea, but also a very expensive ring.

When Dr. Wright told some friends of the incident, one of them exclaimed: "What a dirty trick!" Is it, however, any worse than what some so-called Christians do when over their coffee cups they drop the poison of prejudice, malice, and lies in their remarks concerning someone who is not present?

Ideas like this can be used to provoke earnest thinking on the part of some who may never have realized the terror of malicious gossip. Historical illustrations can open the eyes of our minds and etch vivid images upon our memories.

Kahlil Gibran's *The Madman: His Parables and Poems,* for instance, concerns the terror of unconfessed hatred. Gibran says that in the town where he was born lived a woman and her daughter, both of whom walked in their sleep. One night when everything was bathed in silence, the woman and her daughter, "walking, yet asleep, met in the mist-veiled garden." The mother said: "At last, at last, my enemy! You by whom my youth was destroyed, who have built up your life upon the ruins of mine! Would I could kill you!" The daughter's judgment of her mother was just as harsh: "O hateful woman," she exclaimed, "selfish and old! who stands between my freer self and me! who would have my life an echo of your own faded life! Would you were dead!" At the very moment they finished speaking, a cock crew. This awakened both women. Speaking very gently, the mother said, "Is that you, darling?" And just as gently the daughter answered, "Yes, dear!"

4. Divine Mercy

Normally our imagination must be quickened if we feel the force of, and respond to, the appeal of divine mercy. And so we may begin by quoting Shakespeare's lines:

The quality of mercy is not strain'd;
It droppeth as the gentle rain from heaven
Upon the place beneath: it is twice bless'd;
It blesseth him that gives and him that takes:
'Tis mightiest in the mightiest; it becomes
The throned monarch better than his crown;

. . . .

It is an attribute to God Himself.

We may continue the illustration with the story of John Masefield's *Everlasting Mercy*. We can picture the poacher Saul Kane, cruel, drunk, vile. Then came the beckoning purity of a woman, who finally led this transgressor into the court of heaven. Quite effectively we can quote Saul Kane when he said that he "neither thought" nor did he "strive." Rather, he yielded himself to God, and thus peace came to him. The bolted door had actually "broken in. . . . I knew that I had done with sin."

5. INTERNATIONAL RELATIONS

In his pulpit messages the minister will be dealing with the religious interpretation of our international relationships. He may point out that undoubtedly one of the reasons for the failures of the United Nations is the fact that people will not cultivate the capacity to understand each other. We refuse to project ourselves into the situations and feelings of others. We are eager for people to understand us, but we do not take time to appreciate their viewpoint, their attitude, their background. Historical imagination demands a knowledge of history, an appreciation of national traditions, and a mental grasp of those circumstances which we are prone to believe "circumscribe others." We fail to see that our unwillingness to appreciate and understand other people is but another indication of how narrow and little we ourselves are, both mentally and spiritually.

George Bernard Shaw seems to have been thinking of this when he prophesied that the United Nations would probably fail. The major reason he gave is that the members of different national groups do not understand each other's languages. They have not taken time to state their ideas in the simple phraseology of porters, red caps, and household servants. Doubtless, however, a deeper explanation for this specific failure to learn how to use plain, short words is in the fact that we do not make an honest effort to understand each other's *history, background, mental milieu* and all the *contemporary circumstances* which seriously affect men's lives. We refuse to see what other people see and to feel what they feel. This is obviously one of the main barriers between Western civilization and the Oriental world.

Certainly all who are Christians will be eager to develop imagination in our economic relationships, especially as these affect employers and employees. This has to do with the capacity to put themselves in each other's place and then with what Paul called *agape*—love—go out to bridge the chasms that separate one group from the other. Sir William Beveridge, of the London School of Economics, was dealing with this lack of imagination when he declared that "strikes and lockouts and other industrial stoppages could be put to an end pretty quickly if employers and employees would try to put themselves in thought and imagination in each other's point of view." Indeed, all of us must learn to look at both people and programs through the eyes of Christian understanding.

Hence, we ask, Why race to the moon when we have not yet learned how to live on earth? Why spend billions on space ships when millions in India and Southeast Asia are hungry? If we have insight enough to see that techniques are being emphasized more than concern for human beings, we have a relevant and vital message for this day.

Take a glance also at "man-made man." Electronics may give us better eyes than human beings can claim and finer memories than any of us possess. But no "scientific progress" can give any person appreciation, awe, worship, and love.

35

V. How to Cultivate Imagination

Each minister must learn for himself the best methods of cultivating his imagination. There are so many techniques that none of us need completely fail. This is our hope in a day of mass communication with all it may mean.

Here is a friend who tells of his habit of going into the pulpit at least once during the week and looking out upon the empty pews before him, but with the vision of a congregation at worship. These are the people whose names he knows, who are under his pastoral care. As he faces the empty church, by means of a vivid imagination he plans how to speak best and most effectively to his people in his Sunday morning sermon.

Reading particular books is most effective in cultivating this talent. Ponder the contents of *House of Dolls*.[4] Based on the diary of a young Jewess who was arrested in Poland when she was fourteen, the book tells of her subjection to enforced prostitution in a Nazi labor camp. This terrifying story shows the depth to which hosts under Hitler sank. It also discloses what can happen to anyone or any group without divine resources.

Thus by imagination we go where our people live, where they find happiness, where they suffer. Above all, we go daily to the top of Calvary to see the world and its people as Christ saw them. We learn what Jesus meant when he commended his disciples: "Blessed are your eyes for they see" (Matt. 13:16). Here is imagination, inspiration, and the endowment of God's Holy Spirit.

These gifts of God make it possible for us, as devoted ministers, to underscore the reality of hope for our hearers, many of whom have been defeated by despair. In the blackness of the present night some even find it difficult to see the slightest ray of light which may promise a new dawn.

A sharp sentence by Olive Shreiner, British writer, be-

---

[4]*House of Dolls*, by Ka-tzetnik (Panther Books, London, 1958).

comes relevant. She once said that she would hate to be God. This is not an irreverent statement. Rather it becomes painfully realistic, when we think how few people can see enough to impel them to offer all their talents and capacities to God for the purpose of his creating a new world.

Vividly we are reminded of how important such dedication is, as we recall a classic story concerning a young and ambitious artist who lived in Florence years ago. His flaming purpose was to create from marble a figure which would make him famous. One day a rich friend happily surprised him by bringing to his shop a perfect block of marble from the quarries of Carrara. The artist was overwhelmed with the challenge of this opportunity. But he did not see clearly enough, and when he picked up his chisel, it was only to ruin the stone. He died a discouraged and brokenhearted man.

Then one day Michelangelo passed along and saw that same block of marble. He had it brought to his workshop. Because he had the eye of an artist, as well as the consummate genius of a sculptor, out of that apparently ruined marble he brought forth his masterpiece, "David." Even the artistically dull-minded are stirred deeply by that almost perfect piece of work.

Such a story reminds us that out of this broken world can be created something beautiful. But God depends upon those who have the power of imagination, such as Jesus constantly portrayed. Only those who have the imagination that enables them to feel the presence of God will have either the faith or the courage to try.

When· Christian imagination leads to dedication akin to that of Christ on Calvary, our world will have hope, for God will have a chance through us to save the world. This is the message of the minister who knows how to make his imagination Christian.

III

DISCIPLINED DEVOTION

The preacher of today has more competitors than any other individual who influences the minds of people. Organized religion has never had to face such fierce rivalry, in so many different ways. The minister must have power to pull people away from the Sunday newspaper, the movies, numerous sports, and favorite television programs. He must learn so to hold his hearers' attention that they will not wish they had stayed home to read a book or gone to the club to play golf. Only as he offers something more deeply satisfying than the ordinary engagements of the week end, will he be able to keep people interested enough to continue coming for worship Sunday after Sunday.

Contemporary conditions demand that the preacher personally know spiritual reality. Furthermore, he must be able to present and interpret religion in a vivid, convincing, and appealing way. He will have to show that religion is relevant in the twentieth century. Many worshipers are seeking help for severe and pressing problems. The skill to offer aid is both a science and an art. It necessitates learning rules, following intellectual disciplines, emphasizing moral devotion, and cultivating ethical insight. Obviously these experiences and talents are expensive. But, then, *nothing great comes cheap.*

To some degree, however, we can develop any essential capacity if we are willing to pay the price. This fact presents both a hope and a challenge at a time when much of our religion still seems to be under the spell of Rousseau's philosophy. In advocating the removal of rigid rules in the training of youth, he became a forerunner of the cult of comfort so popular now. Children, he said, should be permitted to make their own choices. The bent of their desires should determine what they do. Many young people themselves have sensed that something was wrong with this idea. There is a story, doubtless historical, concerning a child who, having grown quite irritable doing as he pleased, earnestly requested his parents not to compel him to choose his own schedule day after day.

Now, when we seem to be swept along by social and political tides of such force that we feel we cannot swim against them, we are beginning to see that resignation is not possible for the man of God. Certainly neither relaxation of moral standards nor surrender to the enemies of Christian ethics will be considered seriously by those whose daily disciplines are the result of devotion to "that strange Man on the Cross."

Sooner or later, we learn that discipline has always been necessary for accomplishing any worthy purpose. *We cannot do as we please if we please to do anything worth doing.* Capricious choices and the development of character do not go together. Any high aim requires loyalty of mind and heart. Noble causes make rigid demands. Although no one should understand this better than the Christian minister, every area of life demonstrates the validity of this truth.

I. TRAINING FOR ATHLETICS

Manifestly, discipline is necessary for physical training. One of the great baseball pitchers of all time, Christy Matheson, knew this. As a boy he dreamed of becoming famous. But he did not merely daydream.

Young Christy entered into trades with boys in the neighborhood, offering his prized possessions for their baseballs. When he had a pailful of them, he proceeded to cut a hole in the shed which stood on the back of the lot. With marked care he made this opening the exact width of home plate, carving it as high from the ground as are an ordinary man's knees and extending it up to the level of the average man's shoulders. Thousands of times he threw balls through this opening, continuing to practice until he was able to throw one ball after the other through the hole in the wall. After that, he began throwing curves. This discipline finally made him a great pitcher and brought his record to baseball's Hall of Fame. Other athletes have followed the same rigid rules of training because they earnestly coveted some skill.

The pattern is the same for saints. They will not be deterred or detoured from their purpose. They are dedicated to truth and character, to learning and love. So must the preacher give himself to all that is Godlike if he is to have a word to which people will give heed in a day of disillusionment and doubt.

II. ARTISTIC AND MENTAL MASTERY

Artistic and mental training, involving the development of any personal talents, demands the same basic discipline.

Jenny Lind reminds us of how important it is to begin our education and habits of study as early as possible. When she was only three years of age, she went to visit her grandmother, whose home was near the border of Sweden. Fascinated by the bugles which she heard each morning, Jenny climbed upon the piano stool and began picking out the notes of the bugle call. Fortunately, Jenny's grandmother recognized the signs of authentic musical talent. Thus what might have been considered a nuisance became the happy beginning of long years of fixed habits in studying music. Without this discipline Jenny Lind would never have become "the Swedish nightingale."

Right habits put heart in what we are doing. Without this disciplined devotion, we miss the greatest values of life and of our profession. Richard S. Emrich is quite correct when he insists that "only an age inwardly complacent, superficially optimistic," could say the nonsensical things about the religious disciplines which are being suggested by so many people. Not only in religion is discipline lacking, as the university student made evident when he declared that he had at last got his schedule in perfect shape He did not have a class before ten o'clock in the morning, and every lecture was on the first floor!

Certainly the minister's task makes such demands that he must become devoted to the hours of daily study. Besides preaching there are many other skills he must learn and numerous activities in which he will have to engage. If, however, he does not know how to preach, he may not get the chance to participate in the others.

Of course, we are pastors, or shepherds, as well as preachers. But as an English minister says, being a shepherd is not "the same thing as being a sheep dog." It does not mean that we are "fussing around" the congregation in the morning when we should be in earnest study, learning the methods and the message for the sermon on Sunday. If we major in the minors, and thus foolishly magnify ourselves instead of our commission, thinking that we must constantly be with people day in and day out, we may have little opportunity to magnify the Son of God by an effective message when we enter our pulpits. It was necessary for Christ to withdraw from the crowds in order to bring a message of impelling power when he returned.

There is no substitute for disciplined devotion. Paul exhorts his friends in Philippi: "Finally, brethren, whatsoever things are true, whatsoever things are honest, whatsoever things are just, whatsoever things are pure, whatsoever things are lovely, whatsoever things are of good report; if there be any virtue, and if there be any praise, think on these things" (Phil. 4:8). If the true, the good, and the lovely are ever to become a vital part of our mental processes, we shall have to pursue them and seek to incarnate them. Today when we must have an authentic word for frightened people, Paul's directions constitute a *sine qua non* for the minister who plans to demonstrate that courageous living is practical and possible.

III. Ministers Who Become Masters

We must cultivate these mental disciplines at the outset of our training. We who deal with youth should learn early to let God fashion our own characters.

Consider Frederick W. Robertson, who died when he was only thirty-seven. Because he constantly lived with the poets, he could give quickly the gist of a notable passage or quote a striking phrase. "Conscience does make cowards," "dim religious light," and many other classic descriptions came as a result of his familiarity with Shakespeare, Milton, Coleridge, Wordsworth, and Tennyson. It was his disciplined devotion to literature which kept him constantly awake to the finest thoughts of his day.

The text Robertson chose for the short sermon which the candidate for ordination rites was required to deliver was particularly appropriate for the occasion. It revealed the alert attitude he constantly cultivated. "Awake, thou that sleepest, and arise from the dead, and Christ shall give thee light." This alertness, he felt, was "peculiarly characteristic of a minister's distinctive mission." Because he kept himself mentally awake, thousands found in his sermons "a living source of impulse, a practical direction of thought, a key to many of the problems of theology, and above all a path to spiritual freedom." He had learned to endure hardness, as well as to guide his life by habits of earnest study. He could have made his own the testimony of J. Bronowski, contemporary scientist: "I read greedily, with excitement, with affection, with a perpetual sense of discovering a new and, I slowly realized, a great literature."[1]

Charles H. Spurgeon illustrates the same principles of earnest thinking and constant study in order to relate religion to practical matters. He would ask a housewife as she was kneading bread, "Have you tasted the bread of life?" Stopping to talk with a carpenter, at an appropriate

---

[1] *The Common Sense of Science* (Pelican Books, London), p. 7.

moment he would ask, "Have you ever tried to build a house on sand?" He borrowed illustrations from the London traffic and the London fog, from the poor and the ordinary men and women who faced life's difficult hours.

Because he was diligent in his own youth, Spurgeon knew that lives could be fashioned by God. See what this has often meant:

> I took a piece of living clay
> And gently formed it day by day,
> And moulded with my power and art
> A young child's soft and yielding heart.
> I came again when days were gone—
> He was a man I looked upon;
> He still that early impress wore,
> And I could change him nevermore.[2]

Disciplines are not the same for all preachers, for both physical equipment and spiritual talents vary. Philip Melanchthon was frail physically, and yet he gave us his best work about the same time the "bluff and hearty fighter," Martin Luther, was making his notable contribution to the Reformation.

And who can forget George MacDonald? Disturbed by diseased lungs and harassed by poverty, he held himself to diligent study. He has influenced many thousands who have never known his name. C. S. Lewis, the most widely read lay writer in the field of religion today, unhesitatingly admits that George MacDonald has colored his thinking more than has any other one man.

How different was Henry Ward Beecher! And yet how similar in his devotion to regular habits of study. Living in a critical day of American history, he shows us how to communicate effectively in any crisis. He read histories and then described the movements of God through the

---

[2]"The Teacher," author unknown. See Frank H. Leavell, *The Master's Minority* (Broadman Press, Nashville, 1949), p. 157.

centuries. He read the poets, and their words became sweet perfume. He was determined to know the dramatists. This is how he was himself able to dramatize truth so vividly. Even when he spoke of the deepest matters of life his people responded eagerly and happily. Some have called him a genius. If he was, Beecher was a genius who knew how to work.

So was John Wesley—preaching, praying, or writing practically all the time. There was not an hour in the day that he did not plan with assiduous care, because of his devotion to his "classes" and his Christ.

If someone suggests that these men lived in a day of greater leisure than is ours, let him turn immediately to Archbishop William Temple. Modern inventions and a highly complicated schedule did not interfere with his training. Handicapped with congenital cataract on the right eye, he wore special glasses. He read so slowly that he himself indicated it was "at the pace at which I can pronounce all the words separately, doing that pretty fast." Yet the prodigious reading which he did included philosophy, theology, history, sociology, biography. He was fond of detective stories and books by such writers as John Buckan, Dorothy Sayers, Angela Thirkell, Ann Bridge, and J. B. Priestly.

"Life," he penned in a note in 1931, "is rather hectic! If I do get a clear half hour I write the next bit of Saint John instead of personal letters." His reference is to the Gifford Lectures, many parts of which were written in these "clear half hours." When we who want to let God speak through us accept rules like these, we will gain some ability to handle truth with scientific accuracy.

We must measure our dedication by no standard lower than that of the devotees of communism, who have a philosophy, a program, and a passion! If we do less than they, we shall never begin to understand the searching words of Christ, "What do ye more than others?" (Matt. 5:47).

IV. Dedication Means Discipline

No one ever "leaps" into anything even distantly resembling effectiveness as a writer or speaker. At a fashionable dinner Lord Northcliff impressed this truth upon a society matron who was seated by him. In that superficial conversational vein which too frequently characterizes such occasions, this woman exclaimed, "It's perfectly wonderful how everyone is reading about that man Thackeray. Just to think, he hadn't been heard from a fortnight ago. Why, he awoke one morning and found himself famous."

"Madam," replied Lord Northcliff, "on the morning that Thackeray woke up and found himself famous he had been writing eight hours a day for fifteen years. The man who wakes up and finds himself famous hasn't been asleep, my dear lady."

If someone says there have been exceptions, suggesting that Rip van Winkle seems to contradict the principle, let him remember that this character became famous neither as a writer nor as a pioneer in activities for social righteousness. As a matter of fact, he became famous simply because he had slept through a revolution, and that no Christian minister can dare do!

The cult of comfort has, to be sure, controlled the thinking of thousands of churchmen. We have "cushioned our pews, softened our lights, shortened our sermons, adjusted our hours of service to interfere as little as possible with the other activities of our pleasure-loving parishioners." When this happens, however, Christianity is abandoned.

Although no one of us really has the right to speak upon such themes as "Complete Dedication," and "The Challenge of the Cross," we cannot avoid using such ideas. They belong to the essence of the gospel. We dare use them, however, only as we offer ourselves in dedication to the greatest cause which has ever challenged mankind.

Arturo Toscanini points the direction in which every artist, scientist, and preacher must travel if he becomes effective. His well-known philosophy is suggested by the succinct summary: "Democracy in life, aristocracy in music." Once after showing his musicians how they could improve, he shóuted: "So, you *can* play stronger. Why didn't you do it in the first place? Are you asleep? Have you no respect, no feeling for music? Look at me," he cried; "look at this old man!" In the meantime he was giving himself resounding thumps on the chest. "I give everything—all of myself."[3]

Here, then, is the spirit of the Christian minister: I am going to do my best work in preparing my sermon. I know there are rules of good work as well as of righteous living. They are indispensable during a revolution made possible by disciplined scientists. Because I am dealing with both minds and hearts, I shall seek the same devotion in my "workshop" that my hearers know is necessary in cultivating scientific knowledge. If I help them to decide for Christ, to cultivate Christlike characteristics, I, too, must discipline myself. I hear the ringing challenge of people—and of Christ. To this I respond with heartfelt devotion.

---

[3]*Saturday Review*, March 25, 1950.

IV

PRINCIPLES OF PROCEDURE

Certain basic procedures are necessary for any preacher who hopes to become effective in his pulpit ministry. These become even more important when men are preaching under the pressure of crises. Some of these procedures are so vitally related to the use of homiletical material and the presentation of challenging purposes that all wise students will learn them. Always the minister with spiritual insight will discipline himself rigidly in studying laws that lead to liberty in proclaiming the evangel.

I. A RECORD OF OUR READING

Whatever our age, past experience, or scholastic background, it is necessary to make a record of ideas, poems, illustrations, quotations, and numerous facts *at the time they come to us.* Only so shall we have them at hand when we need them most.

In his *Brief Life of Hobbes*,[1] John Aubrey reminds us that this writer walked a great deal while he meditated. He always carried a pen and inkhorn in the head of his staff. He also kept a notebook in his pocket, and when any helpful thought flashed into his mind, immediately he entered it into his book. He was fearful of losing it unless he recorded it at the moment the thought reached him. This is the secret of what Clement F. Rogers[2] calls the "clear and original, if often mistaken, thought" of this master. Certainly it is the first secret that every preacher must learn if he anticipates having adequate homiletical material for any occasion. It is just as necessary if he hopes to under-

---

[1] See discussion by Clement F. Rogers, in *The Parson Preaching* (Macmillan Company, New York), p. 5.
[2] *Ibid.*

stand what others have said or be equipped to write his own thoughts clearly for the sake of his congregation. This is a discipline which may become both a science and an art. For the effective preacher, it is now more vital than ever before.

Let us imagine that we are angered by the sharp criticisms of the Christian philosophy of life so vigorously presented by Joseph Wood Krutch. Suddenly our hearts leap with excitement. For when he writes of ours being the most successful generation that ever existed, he goes on to add that we have gained *goods* without discovering what is *good.*[3] Joseph Wood Krutch does not claim to be a Christian, but he sees quite clearly some things many church people have not been willing to face.

Again, a minister is reading *Declaration of Freedom,*[4] by Elton Trueblood. He stops to ponder these words: "Those who really believe in the free way of life are bound to seek to make it prevail. . . . We are bound to share what we truly prize."

Obviously this whole problem must be related to Christian missions. Immediately we have a sermon and it is ours, for we follow through with our own thinking. Although there must be days of diligent study before us, already we know where we are going. We are happily aware that Christianity is a religion of concern for the welfare of all people. Of course, we are not to *force* others to believe. We speak the truth and eagerly ask divine Love to guide our words and control our attitudes. This is the evangel. Understanding what this means, we have the heart of our sermon. We are ready to proceed with the idea *that all Christians are missionaries.* We are witnesses, sent to declare and demonstrate the redemptive grace and power of God.

As we record quotations with reference to this or other topics we are careful to quote completely and accurately.

[3]See *Human Nature and the Human Condition* (Random House), pp. 3ff.
[4]Harper and Brothers, 1955, p. 13.

This is one of the greatest timesaving devices that any writer can learn. If we fail here and later discover we have only a phrase or a brief summary, the probability is that we shall not have adequate facts for an accurate quotation. The feeling that we will remember the full and complete reference without recording it is one of the most deceiving emotions of our professional life. Certainly we can adopt our own shorthand methods, but we must know what we are going to use, as well as how and why—as far as we can at the moment.

II. QUESTIONS TO ASK

Again we will not merely quickly file the ideas which come to us; we will insistently ask what the *implications* of these ideas are and *how* we may use them in sermons. Whenever a thought worthy of a sermon comes to us, we can seek the wisest possible answer to these questions. Even if we are engaged in pastoral visitation, we can stop long enough to record the idea and anticipate its use later. We will ask, "What did the writer say? What does he really mean? What would be the ultimate result of his philosophy? What can his ideas mean for my congregation?"

Some evening we are reading Thomas Merton. These sentences etch themselves on our minds: "Charity is neither weak nor blind. . . . It is clear, then, that to love others well we must first love the truth. . . . Charity makes me seek far more than the satisfaction of my own desires, even though they be aimed at another's good. . . . In order to love others with perfect charity I must be true to them, to myself, and to God."[5]

Our sense of direction is quite clear. We may neither agree with all of Merton's theology nor feel that his monastic order adequately represents practical Christianity. Nevertheless, here is something so vital and thought-pro-

---

[5] In *No Man Is an Island* (Harcourt, Brace and Co., New York, 1955), pp. 6, 7, 8.

49

voking that we stop to recall the familiar words of Jesus: "Ye shall know the truth and the truth shall make you free. . . . If any man will come after me, let him . . . take up his cross and follow me" (John 8:32; Matt. 16:24).

Another day our attention is arrested by the headline of an Associated Press story, date-lined Meyers Mill, South Carolina. The correspondent states that the Meyers Mill Baptist Church "ended 121 years of service today to make way for development of the huge Savannah River H-bomb project." The incident immediately focuses our attention on this question: Are we substituting hydrogen power for spiritual power?

The story suggests conditions which we must frankly face. This single incident vividly dramatizes world conditions with which we can deal satisfactorily only in the light of the purpose and power of God. Thus do we meditate upon the relationship of facts to faith—facts we observe and faith that holds us secure.

One morning in our study we vividly recall how multitudes—without the least flippant or superficial attitude—have asked, What happens after death? What is the good of science if it cannot tell us this? Certainly the earnest desire of most church people when they are thinking clearly or facing life's crises, or as today are aware of the imminent danger of global destruction, is to know whether life has meaning, and if so, what it is.

Thus, day after day, as we record references and materials which later we anticipate using in various sermons, we will keep in mind what we hope to do with what we have. This is part of any method of procedure for effective preaching.

Remembering that most men worry because they do not believe in God, that is, a God like Christ, and knowing that sometime we shall have to deal with this issue, as alert preachers we record historical and contemporary incidents which will be relevant to this theme. We think of Gloucester in *Lear*, who was lacking in Christian faith.

We remember words Thomas Hardy placed on the lips of one of his characters, "The president of the immortals had finished his sport with Tess." Or again, we see this sentence, "As flies to wanton boys are we to the gods—they kill us for their sport." But we also remember that many people have faced dangerous and difficult days without losing their faith. Such a philosophy becomes even more relevant during an intellectual revolution, accompanied by international crises.

Meditating on the practical way we can make faithfulness and faith vivid and real, our minds become receptive to pertinent facts. Thus one morning in our devotions, we are reading the account of those faithful Hebrews whose story is carried in the Book of Daniel. We remember our reading of *Tom Brown's School Days*. Here is the English version of a boy who had the nerve to stand against ridicule.

A new boy came to a room in which there were twelve beds and twelve boys. The first night he spent in this school, he knelt down to say his prayers. Tom Brown turned his head just in time to see a heavy slipper flying through the air, aimed for the head of this kneeling boy. When the lights were out later, Tom Brown remembered his own mother and the prayers she had taught him—prayers he had never used since he came to Rugby. Then and there he made a decision that the next evening he, too, would kneel to pray. And so, his fellow students were amazed to see Tom Brown, one whom they respected and feared, kneel down beside his bed to pray.

The story is old, but the principle is not outdated. Again we face the same test. When millions think we have outgrown religion, we are to demonstrate its eternal qualities and character. Is Christianity this important in the latter part of this twentieth century? Here is our searching question. We have to give some answer.[6]

There is a morning when we are thinking of prayer.

---

[6]For a more complete discussion, see *Religion That Is Eternal*, Chapter I, (Macmillan, 1960).

Many ideas will come to mind. We will write them clearly. We recall that prayer is an art which involves certain carefully followed techniques. There is always *preparation, contemplation* of the Deity, an attitude of *expectancy,* and some kind of helpful *results* for those who understand what it is to engage in sincere and unhurried thoughts of the Divine.

III. TESTS FOR THE TRUTHS WE PREACH

Whether we are seeing some great truth for the first time, planning how we will use a newly discovered illustration, or are seriously at work in our study on the next pulpit message, there is another basic truth which we must constantly face. It is this: The effectiveness of any sermon is necessarily determined by its dependability. If the message we preach is not dependable, people will either pay it no attention or soon abandon it.

The importance of facing up to the severe tests most of us eventually meet was suggested by an incident during the hurricane of 1938 in New England. It was feared that the railroad bridge at White River Junction would be swept away since apparently there was no way to make it secure. At the suggestion of a keen-minded engineer, a long line of heavily loaded freight cars were backed onto the bridge. The bridge stood, helped by the weight it bore. So must our religion—even when the crises are most severe. The people who hear us must feel confident that the truth we present will stand the severest kind of strain. Such confidence makes the gospel meaningful. Our hearers become aware that God is their source of strength. Their security —and ours—is in him, not in bomb shelters or fall-out shelters.

A newspaper story suggests how utterly inadequate any other power is, as it also emphasizes the eternal importance of resources that will never fail. Dr. Kalervo Oberg, of the Smithsonian Institute, vividly describes his visits to the Nambiguara and Terena tribes who live deep in the

Amazon jungles. They are suspicious of white men, as many other natives of South America are. One of the big worries of this particular group, Dr. Oberg tells us, is that their military secrets might be revealed. As soon as any stranger approaches, they hide their bows and arrows. We smile at this fear, but it is possible that our attempts to keep our nuclear secrets from other groups in the world will sometime be just as humorous.

Actually the scholars will find that these two tribes have "considerable culture." Living in a relatively unexplored area in a dense forest, they find a fairly satisfactory existence possible by living near "the banks of rivers which form the headwaters of the Amazon."

We may condescendingly refer to their naiveté, but we are immediately compelled to ask: "What is our own idea of power?" Obviously the word "primitive" is relative, and ultimate reality is to be found only in divine resources.

There are certainly no military secrets which can save any nation or any civilization. "Our help is in the name of the Lord" (Ps. 124:8). The psalmist who wrote or sang these words knew the open secret of those who will be saved. Our weapons are spiritual, as Paul pointed out. They have to do with Christian character. No material or secular aid is adequate. "God is our refuge and strength" (Ps. 46:1). Christians have gained even more confidence that "the Lord of hosts is with us" (vs. 11); that he "is able to do exceeding abundantly above all that we ask or think" (Eph. 3:20).

Dr. Olin F. Stockwell, a missionary imprisoned by the Communists in China for twenty-three months, learned the deeper meaning of these words in a specific way. He was in solitary confinement most of his imprisonment. Three things made it possible for him to survive and not collapse nervously, he tells us: the New Testament, the grace of God, and a sense of humor.

Now he looks back upon this restriction of his freedom as a time when he received numerous valuable spiritual insights. Even in the communist prison he remained creative. He made a collection of talks, poems, and articles that he could use out of prison. This ambassador of Christianity proved that life is what God and we make it, even though it may include the uncertainties, privations, and loneliness of a communist prison.

IV. PROCEEDING WITH TRUTH THAT MEETS HUMAN NEED

So we proceed with truth that not merely searches the hearts of our hearers, but at the same time gives them assurance that it will meet their deepest needs. In a subtle way O. Henry has suggested the importance of acquiring a basis for such assurance before personal crises strike. Writing of a thief who sat smoking a big cigar, he describes how comfortable the man felt. Life seemed rosy for him. Apparently he was quite successful. He had tricked a simple-minded old man out of a wad of money. The eyes of this successful thief were set in fat. As he smiled, he seemed· to exude complete contentment. Everything was manifestly just right for him.

Then the unexpected occurred. As he looked up, he saw a young woman hurrying home. She was dressed in plain white. He had known the young lady years before, when they were school children together. The two of them had sat on the same bench at school and shared many hours as comrades. The thief got up. He could not stand either the sight or the thought of this young woman. Laying his face against the cool iron of a lamppost, he exclaimed, "God, I wish I could die!" It is painfully obvious that he had not found the secret of great living.. There are multitudes like him. By means of the evangel, we can bring them a dependable message of hope—the evangel of the New Testament.

Children, as well as adults, must see the worth of devotion to Christian causes. To commend what some youth has done for the sake of Christ may be a far more effective means of winning their dedication than is condemnation or even mere affirmation of the value of commitment to high purpose.

During Holy Week a few years ago in one of our smaller cities, two major league baseball teams played an exhibition game. So successful was the program of advertising that even the public schools announced that permission would be given children to attend the game, provided they brought written requests from their parents. A boy, with the enthusiasm which often characterizes youth, had become so interested in the Holy Week services at his church that he asked his mother why the schools did not accept written permissions which would excuse students for the purpose of attending a one-hour service of worship being conducted each morning at the church to which he belonged. Many of us felt like asking, "Why not?"

Turning to another area vital to contemporary political crises, we know that, in spite of the problem of separation of church and state, when public education tends to minimize the importance of religion, our nation is facing imminent danger. Secularism is a serious problem. Earnest study is demanded when materialism is magnified as it is in the Western world. We must be able to supply proof that youth *can be challenged.* Beyond this, we must be able to show that enthusiastic devotion to the church and the cause of Christ is even more important than interest in athletics or social affairs. Manifestly we who are privileged to direct the thinking of those who worship in our churches will act very foolishly if we fail to magnify every expression of interest and of loyalty.

Certainly we who preach must be concerned enough for the welfare of mankind that we dare to speak for those who are now oppressed, or who have never had a fair chance. G. A. Studdert Kennedy felt this keenly when he blazed out in anger in defense of the defenseless. One of his favorite themes was "The Sorrow and Suffering of God." When a critic suggested that Kennedy was then dealing

with a metaphysical question, and moreover, was needlessly reviving a heresy of the early days of Christianity,
Kennedy insisted that he had to show God to men in the
trenches in a way in which they could understand. Meta-
physics did not primarily concern him. He had to make
soldiers see a God who could command their respect and
win their love. Why, he asked, should any doctrine considered a heresy in the fourth century necessarily be a
heresy in the twentieth?

Studdert Kennedy was certain that the ultimate terms
by which he was to value anything were the standards of
Christ. No wonder even unbelievers who heard this prophet
of God never felt that he was discussing some irrelevant
theme. They never accused him of "dragging in" religion.
This preacher knew too well where people lived—mentally
and spiritually—to make that mistake.

V. MAKING LIFE WORTH LIVING

Knowing that Jesus constantly spoke of values that make
men want to live abundantly, as he prepares his sermon
the Christian minister will be eager to show *why* men
need a source of divine strength and *how* they can find it.
Often he will recall the painful earnestness of Macbeth's
appeal to his physician:

> *Canst thou not minister to a mind diseas'd;*
> *Pluck from the memory a rooted sorrow;*
> *Raze out the written troubles of the brain;*
> *And with some sweet oblivious antidote*
> *Cleanse the stuff'd bosom of that perilous stuff*
> *Which weighs upon the heart?*

Macbeth, of course, is compelled to listen to the doctor's
sad words, "Therein the patient must minister to himself."
The physician could not heal the sinful soul of Lady Macbeth. But we, as Christian ministers, know One who can.

The sermons we preach, therefore, will contain such dependable truth that our people become sure there is healing for hurt minds, cleansing for sinful souls, and strength for daily living. Such messages do not need a blood transfusion!

As we continue the writing of the sermon, we will constantly keep the Christlike God at the center of our thinking. In his essay on Robert Burns, Dr. Stopford Brooke searchingly depicts the tremendous importance of this centrality of Christ. He reminds us how "the Christian ministers of Aryshire had blotted out Christ for Burns." Thus they threw the poet back, unhelped, upon himself. Of course they should not have failed so tragically. *They need not have missed their chance.* Nor do we have to repeat the same mistake.

Certainly, steadfast assurance is not thrust upon us. Often we must travel a long road before we find it. But when we sincerely and intelligently accept Christ, we proceed with that confidence which is indispensable in a day of widespread doubt and pronounced religious difficulty.

Thus every principle of procedure is vitally relevant to sermons that make clear the goodness and strength of God —his ability and desire to respond to our deepest needs.[7]

---

[7]See discussion of "To Whom We Pray" in author's *Prayer That Prevails,* (Macmillan, New York, 1958).

V

THE PREACHER BECOMES HIS OWN INQUISITOR

For the first few years of his ministry every preacher ought to ask himself a number of questions either before he begins the writing of his sermon or during the writing of it. For the young man who hopes to become an effective preacher, this discipline is practically a necessity. If he delays this personal examination until the completion of the first draft, it may be too late. Even later in his ministry, after he has disciplined himself to search his mind almost automatically or subconsciously, he will realize the wisdom of raising certain questions relative to the sermon—its purpose, plan, and ultimate effect. When anyone is quite sure that he knows all the disciplines of the mind, he is obviously in most danger; for no writer can ever know too well how to prepare his manuscript.

What makes this discipline so vital, even essential, at this time, is the fact that we cannot afford to lose a single hour of opportunity to make plain and persuasive the message of the gospel. We who preach during a revolution are under the compulsion of being sure that every sermon shines with relevant truth and is directed to needs world-wide as well as to those which are intimately personal.

Those who are most alert—both young ministers and we who are older—will be eager to learn positive directions which only searching questions mark with clarity. That is why the term "inquisitor" is none too strong.

A study of outstanding athletes discloses the same necessary mental discipline. Bobby Jones began to learn golf when he was so small his father had to buy him special clubs, suitable for a young boy. With the curiosity of a child he found it easy to ask many questions relevant to the game. By the time he was a young man on the golf course, Bobby knew the basic principles of how to swing a club, the art of following through, and the minutiae of rules which the novice must learn. The day came when he did not have to ask himself *how* to swing each time he took a stroke. But even after he was world famous there were days he did question himself, "What did I do wrong?" and "How can I get more distance?"

Some time ago I traveled across a state to see a young college student play basketball, because he, too, had set high standards of excellence for himself. He was only six feet tall—a low height for a basketball player when so many coaches seek men who can both control the ball off the backboards and gain the "jump" on competitors. Yet this young man made All-American as a guard. One of the main reasons was that when he was only a child he began learning the answers to vital questions. Again and again he asked how he could throw a basketball through a hoop and control the play of the ball with hands and movement of feet. He learned how to weave back and forth across a court by asking hundreds of times what mistakes he had made and then correcting them.

An interview his coach gave reporters was carried by the Associated Press. It dealt with the eagerness of this young man. This devotee of the game was always the first player on the floor in the afternoon, even before the time scheduled for practice. When the other players had gone, he was still practicing. Reading the criticism of sports writers to the effect that there was one skill which he had failed to develop, the lad did not become incensed with his critics. He asked himself, How can I learn this? Then he began throwing the ball from the proper angle, asking over and over how to execute the play with efficiency, until he had mastered it. He also became an All-American baseball player in college and went directly from the campus to the majors.

Only the preacher who desires to become effective is of

any worth for this day. He will insistently raise vital questions concerning his sermons. He must know what he is writing, how he is speaking, what are the effects of his sermons. Power and persuasion cannot be acquired in any other way. Without this i n s i s t e n t questioning of himself he need not try to speak during these difficult and dangerous days when so many are oppressed with a sense of futility and when his competitors are so unyielding in their demands for his parishioners' interest and time.

I. What Is My Purpose?

As soon as he begins to outline his sermon, the minister should ask himself, "Why am I making this sermon?" If it is only because one is scheduled to preach at ten or eleven o'clock, it would be decidedly preferable to attend the service, lead the congregation in worship, and then announce that he did not have a message worthy of attention that morning. He should frankly confess that no propelling purpose had gripped his mind, and then, quite reverently, ask the congregation to kneel or stand for the final prayer and benediction. The next time that minister announced a service, doubtless all who had heard his straightforward confession would be present. Also their testimony concerning the startling genuineness of their preacher would unquestionably cause many other people to turn toward that church.

Our pursuit of a worthy purpose will, of course, be related to our central aim of helping people make the highest possible decisions—morally, ethically, spiritually. Our general objective may be that of deepening the religious devotion of our people or in some way suggesting the manner and methods by which this goal may be reached. Always we will want our hearers to give Christ complete right of way over their lives. But there should also be specific objectives which confirm and reaffirm this basic Christian reason for the sermon. We may have, to be sure, more than one particular purpose for the same sermon, but there should never be a pulpit message without a special reason which justifies the preacher's procedure.

This need for clarity of purpose becomes more important than ever before now when millions seem to have lost any really great objective and worthy purpose for life. In this day of flaunting of moral standards and widespread disregard for high ethics, the least we can do is to sharpen our listeners' sense of right and wrong.

1. WE EMPHASIZE SOME SPECIFIC TRUTH

Manifestly one of the objectives of every sermon should be to set forth truth. This is so vital to our sermon that we can never ignore it save to our own peril. It is part of the urgency Paul felt when he cried: "Woe is unto me, if I preach not the gospel" (I Cor. 9:16).

Moreover, the message which the Christian preacher presents and underscores must not be merely dependable fact; it must be Christian truth. If someone asks how there can be a difference between truth as such and *Christian* truth, the answer is that of course in one sense of the word there is none. In another sense there *is* a distinction—one which the minister must clearly discern and proclaim. For instance, as worthy as the profession of the instructor in mathematics may be, the minister is not following this pattern. In some special way the Christian preacher presents truth so as to guide his people in the *cultivation of Christian character*. Therefore, even were he to use the subject of mathematics as an illustration, his main endeavor would lead him to suggest basic principles which are relevant to Christian character.

The preacher is under moral obligation to express some definite Christian thought in every sermon. At his best, he will be eager to achieve this major purpose. Therefore, he will continue to ask questions which compel him to consider his objective until he thoroughly understands the primary purpose of this message. Only so can he execute his plans, that is, follow through with the proper patterns of pro-

61

cedure. Is it his desire to assure his congregation that, in spite of the darkness of the present hour, the light of God is still shining? Is he going to tell them that when they are discouraged there is a Power to lift them up, to encourage them and give them strength for life's most severe trials? Then he will build his sermon with this sharply defined purpose in mind. Is he going to say that, though fate seems to rule the world, there is a God in charge of the universe, who is not merely divinely gracious, but whose will is in thoroughgoing accord with the spirit and character of Christ? Then his procedure in outlining his sermon will substantiate and demonstrate this plan. He knows where he is going, what the road is, and how he must travel in order to arrive.

2. We Learn to Create a Mood of Worship

It may be that the preacher desires an atmosphere in which truth can be expressed clearly, both now and later. He will seek to create a mental and spiritual mood that makes this possible. Bitter discussions relevant to racial and economic problems may have disturbed the peace of the congregation. Acting as both pastor and preacher, he seeks an atmosphere in which calm thinking is possible. He is tremendously concerned with friendly and gracious attitudes. He speaks to people who are frightened or angry, who have substituted fear and hatred for love. He may base his message on the words of Jesus, "Peace, be still" (Mark 4:39).

Some other day the particular aim which controls everything the minister says and does is that of helping the congregation render a verdict for Christianity. Earnestly he makes an appeal for Christ and his way of life. The writer of this sermon will permit no phase of his outline and no illustration to encourage a mental detour. Everything he does in preparation for his spoken message will help him move toward his goal. Even in the introduction of the sermon, when the congregation may not yet be keenly aware of the ultimate objective, the speaker will know *why* he is taking each mental step—and *where* it leads. He will understand when and why to proceed both intellectually and spiritually, because he has asked himself searching and insistent questions about his immediate purpose.

Without penetrating inquiries like these, we can never see our goal clearly enough to pursue our homiletical work effectively. *The sermon that does not have a specific purpose ought not to be delivered.* If we enter the pulpit simply because we are scheduled to preach, we will fail. Without a meaningful message, we are not ready to stand before the congregation.

This has always been true, but the crises of our day make it imperative. Indeed, the lack of direction and the confusion in the minds of so many people may be, in part, the result of the failure of those of us who preach to have sharply defined, crystal-clear purposes for our sermons.

II. What Are My Talents?

The wise preacher will ask himself a second question: "What can I hope to accomplish?" At first thought this interrogation may seem too closely akin to the one which we have just been considering. There is, however, a very real distinction. The second question compels us to consider *what we are able to do*, and thus forces us frankly to face the fact that there are types and blueprints of sermons which we cannot use as effectively as others.

Certainly we will be eager to study all types and all blueprints, but we shall be aware that we cannot hope to accomplish as much with some methods of procedure as with others. The talents of individuals differ. Hence, we may ask our second question thus: What am I hoping to accomplish and on what facts is this hope based? If I have been trained efficiently in the art of preaching sermons that call for judgment on the evils and injustices of our society and on personal ideals and actions, I should expect results different from those achieved by a man who constantly presents a message which suggests mere psychological techniques for self-management. Indeed, the man who has spent most of his ministry in telling his hearers how easy it is to find peace, poise, and power should not anticipate disturbing the consciences of his hearers as did the prophet Micah or that daring proclaimer of truth, Amos. Such a preacher can hardly hope for results comparable to those of which the name of John the Baptist reminds us. He who has told people that they need never worry about anything cannot reasonably expect results similar to those of a man whose devotion to truth was so great that he finally lost his head. And now, in this atomic age, it is quite clear that the only way we can keep our consciences clear is to deal intelligently with painful facts.

Certainly, if we are wise we will learn how to preach more than one type of sermon. However, we will know that there are some plans, some patterns, which demand more work and cost more "blood, sweat, and tears" than do others.

Furthermore, as preachers, we should recognize the wisdom of using various methods and of emphasizing different phases of the gospel. Consider the testimony recorded by Robert Woodrow in his *Analecta*. He is quoting a merchant whose business had called him to Scotland. Although the incident occurred three hundred years ago, it plainly underscores basic principles relevant for our day. Speaking of Robert Blair, the merchant said, "That man showed me the majesty of God." When he heard Samuel Rutherford, this same visitor to Scotland declared, "That man showed me the loveliness of Christ." As he came away from Irvine, where he had heard a sermon by David Dixon, the churchman exclaimed, "That man showed me all my heart."

Bring the principle closer home. We are agreed that Phillips Brooks was able to do certain things which Henry Ward Beecher never could. P. T. Forsyth did not cultivate the characteristics and style of speaking which made Charles Spurgeon famous. Forsyth probably sought the salvation of his hearers as eagerly as did Spurgeon, but he never reached the poorer people—the unlettered—as did Spurgeon. The latter could hope, therefore, to use certain methods which Forsyth never was able to employ, in spite of his intellectual brilliance.

Comparing and contrasting techniques and methods of various pulpiteers is an effective means of learning both our weak and strong points. This procedure will help us to learn how to answer the question: "What do I have a right to hope to accomplish by means of my sermon?" For instance, Jonathan Edwards could hardly hope to write a sermon which would remind us of Dwight L. Moody. Certainly Moody's hearers did not anticipate being as frightened as people were when they heard Jonathan Edwards' sermon, "Sinners in the Hands of an Angry God."

To be sure, as Thomas DeWitt Talmadge once said, "The human heart is essentially the same in all ages, and the same keys that drew music from it in the days of our fathers will strike responsive chords now." Certainly all the great composers have a contribution for us, and the human heart does respond to the eternal message of music. Furthermore, in this discordant world out of tune with God, we desperately need the music the heavenly host sang at Bethlehem nearly two thousand years ago: "On earth peace, good will toward men" (Luke 2:14).

Of course, we should be keen enough to realize that some musicians do have difficulty with Beethoven, and some who understand Chopin may never master Bach. Indeed, the latter composer may represent the intricately involved type of preaching suggested by the "sermon of paradox." Only an artist can preach understandingly and appealingly this particular type of sermon. This craftsman may say, "I have two texts this morning, the first: 'They that take the sword shall perish with the sword'; the second: 'I am come not to bring peace but a sword.'"

Obviously to deal adequately and satisfactorily with these two apparently contradictory truths requires a much more highly trained specialist than one who uses a thematic type of sermon and simply states, reiterates, and illustrates the particular text and theme which he is eager for his congregation to accept, much as the newspaper editor is compelled to do. Although the preacher who delivers the thematic sermon may present arresting quotations from the philosophers, bits of truth from history, and marshal ringing lines of poetry to substantiate the truth of the sermon, he is using a much simpler and easier type of message to deliver than the sermon of paradox. Knowing the pattern best for us will help us to gain confidence and to become mentally comfortable.

Practical approaches like those suggested here help us to feel "at home" with our congregation. If one is a visiting minister speaking before a group of strangers, he will demonstrate his wisdom by not choosing the kind of sermon most difficult for him. Few of us would appear before a national conference or convention, hoping to present truth effectively, and there use a technique which suggests our marked weaknesses. Certainly when preaching an evangelistic series, we will not choose either technique or blueprint which limits us in fulfilling our essential purpose.

However, if we are wise, we will learn as quickly as we can all possible techniques and methods suitable for proclaiming the good news of the grace of God. Suppose we have found it difficult to preach the sermon of Christian encouragement, one needed today as seldom before. We can study such men as Ian MacLaren, to whom one of his laymen said, "Your best work in the pulpit has been to put heart into men for the coming week."

Yet, as a pulpiteer in his early ministry, before John Watson became world famous as Ian MacLaren, he was practically a failure. When he was at St. Mathew's Church, Charing Cross, Glasgow, one of his elders said of him, "Ah, well, a nice enough young man, but there's nae future in his heid." When the young preacher was leaving for another church, another of his elders in bidding him good-by, shook the hand of his minister cordially and affectionately, saying, "Well, Mr. Watson, I wish you all success. You may be a pastor, but you'll never be a preacher."

The magnificent skills Ian MacLaren later showed underscore the wisdom of being diligent in the study of every possible technique and method. Only so can we hope for the finest results in using an increasingly larger number of sermon types. Some patterns the wise craftsman will never neglect. For instance, although one is adept in presenting the topical sermon, he will cultivate at least some ability as an expository preacher. And certainly the man most proficient as a proclaimer of the social gospel should study earnestly the art of the Christian evangelist.

Now in days when we are being swept by revolutionary forces mightier than we have ever experienced, we remind ourselves that talk is cheaper than ever before and that we have to demonstrate our identity with all who hear us; that we, too, are wrestling with their problems, for they belong to all who desire a Christian society.

III. WHAT STRATEGY SHALL I USE?

A third question which the wise preacher will ask himself is this: "What strategy shall I use in this sermon?" When a man knows his primary purpose and understands, at least to some degree, both his talents and his limitations, this question becomes increasingly vital. A few relevant facts are so important and, at the same time, so simple, that they will throw a flood of light upon others. Obviously, when we plan to preach a "judgment day" sermon, we will not take a text which suggests encouragement. When we have as our purpose to promote reforms, such as those for which Dr. Charles H. Parkhurst once became famous in New York city, manifestly our over-all strategy will not be that which suggests a mood of indulgent relaxation. If, moreover, we are hoping for a Christian counter revolution, we will use every possible means to produce such, including skill and homiletical material.

Strategy is, of course, vital because it has to do with the comprehensive plan of the sermon. It must also be related to the fundamental purpose of the particular sermon which at the moment is being considered. Strategy, therefore, has to do with basic methods, the fundamentals of procedure.

Let us imagine, for instance, that we are dealing with the subject of forgiveness. We are preaching to a group of people who find it difficult to believe that they can be forgiven. Our strategy may be to present quickly, but without any suggestion of haste, a sweep of the centuries recalling the worst sinners who have found forgiveness and experienced such cleansing of their consciences that they have been able to live with themselves. At the moment, whether our text is in the Old or the New Testament is of secondary consequence.

Referring to the Fifty-first Psalm, we may say that although tracing the authorship of this psalm would be helpful in understanding it, such is not essential. Whether the traditional story that the psalm has its origin in a tragic experience in the life of David is accepted, the basic truth remains the same. We may then remind our hearers that David did sin egregiously and afterwards repented with salty tears. Manifestly we have the sincere confession of a man who had sinned and suffered greatly, long before men knew the full terror of sin as it was demonstrated by the Cross.

Then, as we verbally swing across the many years, we may refer to Hosea, pointing out that this man had caught so much of the divine spirit that he was able to offer pardon to one who, humanly speaking, deserved no forgiveness. Then turning to the New Testament to show how Christ forgave Simon Peter after his denial of the Lord, we describe how the look of love in the eyes of Christ called Simon back to his better self.

The bombing of Coventry Cathedral became the occasion of many people's learning more about forgiveness than they had ever known before. One of the many stories which deepened my desire to visit Coventry for the purpose of viewing the widely publicized ruins concerns an evening when one of the ministers of the cathedral found a man kneeling before the altar. His head was bowed, and tears streamed down his cheeks. When he became more composed, he told the clergyman this story: "I was in the German Air Force, and was one who flew over Coventry on that night when this cathedral and so many other things were destroyed. Ever since, my heart has been heavy at the remembrance. Today, as I knelt before this altar and read the words inscribed here, 'Father, Forgive,' something broke within me, and I found release."

IV. What Tactics Shall I Use?

Knowing our over-all strategy and how it is related to the plan of our sermon, we should ask, "What tactics will be effective in accomplishing the purpose of this sermon?" The very fact that it is impossible to separate "tactics" from "strategy" in any literal sense, as the incident just related discloses, serves to underscore the importance of raising each of these issues separately. Actually, all phases of the sermon are vitally related and interrelated, when they emphasize the central purpose of the sermon.

Consider the presentation of the theme which the story about Coventry Cathedral suggests, that is, the forgiving love of God. One of our tactics may be that of dramatic appeal. Alexander Whyte, who made his pulpit in Edinburgh world famous, was able to discuss the forgiving love of God with marked effectiveness, even though he stressed the terror of sin as few ministers have been able to do.

Once when Whyte was describing "the hunting hounds of sin" who were on the trail of the sinner, he cried, "Hark!" At the same moment he lifted his eyes from his manuscript and gazed into the corner behind a young man in the congregation. "Do you not hear?" he asked. "See . . . yon lank, lean-bellied hound making up on you." The young man who described the scene declared that he could not refrain from taking a quick glance over his shoulder!

Undoubtedly Whyte's ability to depict sin with such force gave him extra talent in referring to the "warm, strong, loving arms of the Heavenly Father." To some degree, each of us can develop the same ability, if we feel that our need for God is overwhelmingly great.

Emphasizing the possibility of forgiveness, we may find it necessary to deal with certain individuals who insist they do not need or desire pardon. For now, as always, many people want peace, poise, and power without the personal presence of the holy God. Often we want pardon without the Cross. This, we tell our hearers, cannot be. Some even assert they do not need forgiveness. John Wesley understood this when General Oglethorpe declared, "I never forgive." "Then," Mr. Wesley replied, "I hope, sir, you never sin."

At times many of us exclaim, "Leave us to ourselves!" For all too frequently we want a "wooden Christ" upon a "wooden cross." Nevertheless, we cannot receive the gift of Calvary without walking humbly and gratefully up Golgotha's hill. On our knees we thank God that there heaven met hell for the purpose of saving us. And this we underscore when so many of our hearers wonder if we are only orphans—whether there is any One to help us, any God to save us.

V. WHAT HOMILETICAL MATERIAL SHALL I USE?

We must ask yet another question: "What homiletical material should I use for this sermon?" The answer is manifestly contingent upon the purpose of the sermon as well as upon our strategy and the tactics which we decide to employ. The fact that *purpose, strategy, tactics,* and *content* are interrelated will help to give unity, coherence, and emphasis to the sermon. Indeed, the illustrative material is so vital in making possible a well-integrated sermon, as well as an appealing message, that we will want to weigh the worth of each reference or quotation. Intelligently facing the principles suggested by these interrogations can aid us in learning to use only that material which will throw light on the truth of the text and not draw attention to itself for its own sake.

Of course, when we are wise we become familiar with all phases of life, for all furnish illustrations. We will give particular attention to those types of homiletical material with which we are least familiar. For most of us who preach, science is obviously one of these. Since we daily face the danger of nuclear warfare and possible destruction, made possible by scientific discoveries, we are compelled to give attention to this subject.

But consider also those seminary students and parish ministers who did their undergraduate work in a school of technology, before they planned to enter the ministry. Many who pursued courses in engineering did not major in psychology and philosophy. These they must now study diligently. Because of their academic background, however, they are familiar with many facts in the field of technology or science. Having majored in electricity, chemistry, or physics, they have at hand a wealth of invaluable material.

When we consider our congregation, we prepare sermons including every possible type of homiletical material, emphasizing especially that which may have nothing to do with our profession, but does vitally concern teachers, executives, laborers, housewives, and others in our congregation. Thus will we gain their attention and hold their interest.

So we focus attention on the fact that we need a variety of material, dealing with all professions and areas of life. Suppose we are trying to help develop spiritual alertness and ingenuity on the part of our people. With a delicately humorous touch, we may remind them that most of us are so lacking in imagination that we cannot see how to engage in new and exciting endeavors.

A story comes to mind—one carried by the Associated Press,[1] a few years ago concerning a woman in North Carolina. She wanted to attend a state fair on several days. Because, however, she was reluctant to pay the price of admission each time she came through the gate, she tried to think of some plan that would enable her to visit the fair without so much expense. A bright idea suddenly struck her. Visiting the city market, she bought a large chrysanthemum, paying twenty-five cents for it. This she carried to the fairground, entering it as an exhibit. Because she was an exhibitor, she was permitted a free pass to the fair for the entire week. She had a sticker given her which allowed her free parking. Incidentally, she also won a ribbon and a one-dollar prize for her chrysanthemum!

Again, we may want to show that spiritual ingenuity is vitally related to the attitude of wonder. We recall G. K. Chesterton's insistence that this attribute has atrophied in nearly all of us. He himself, however, went through life startled and astonished at nearly everything he saw. Because he was able to look at things with a "fresh, unjaundiced eye" he became one of the finest creative writers of his day.

The relation of dullness of mind and the refusal to be disturbed by ugliness in life is illustrated by the classic story of an architect who was irritated by the design of a house which he had to pass each day on his way to work. Finally the architect bought the house, moved into it, and continued to live in it, no longer disturbed. Its design never bothered him again; he never saw it!

Approaching the theme of a dull conscience from a different angle, Bishop Francis J. McConnell often told of a visit he made to China a number of years ago. The section of one of the cities in which he resided was frequented by many men who earned their living by pulling rickshas. Because so many of these poor coolies were victims of

---

[1] Related by Sam Ragan in *News and Observer*, Raleigh, North Carolina.

tuberculosis, they were constantly coughing. The Bishop said he was sure that he would never be able to sleep with this coughing going on day and night: cough, cough, cough, cough. He told himself he could not stand it. Actually, though, it required only a few nights for him to become so accustomed to it that he could close his eyes and quickly be lost in slumber.

Though aware of the physical needs of people—constantly presented by newspapers, magazines, movies, and TV—perhaps few Americans react differently from the Bishop. As strange as it may seem, our economic affluence can dull our consciences with respect to the poverty of millions in other parts of the world.

VI. How Can I Help My Hearers Make a Decision?

There is another question the Christian preacher must ask himself: "How can I help my hearers reach a verdict?" If we are to deliver effective messages, we certainly need to learn this skill. The sermon may have to do with our giving to some worthy cause. It may concern generous contributions for the church budget. Possibly it is related to the building of a sanctuary in a distant land. Often it has to do with a deepening of desire for a more complete devotion to Christ. The message may point toward a decision for God, as we accept his will for our lives. Whatever it is, the preacher constantly keeps in mind the specific verdict he wants his hearers to reach.

Certainly we cannot wander mentally or homiletically if we are anticipating a personal commitment on the part of our congregation. Nor can we permit the minds of our people to wander. As quickly and as effectively as possible we will get to the point.

Consider how a visitor to a small town unexpectedly learned the importance of plain, practical procedures. When he alighted at the station, it was late evening. So he went to the railroad agent to learn the way to the home where he was to call. As the station master glanced up, he noticed a man going by his window. "That man is Mr. Brown," he said. "He lives next door to the house to which you desire to go. There is no other building near. Follow Mr. Brown; that will be your easiest way to arrive at your destination."

So it was that the visitor began to walk behind his chosen guide. Soon Mr. Brown became aware that someone was following him. Disturbed, he started walking faster. The stranger quickened his pace. Finally Mr. Brown came to a cemetery which he entered, darting behind tombstones and circling graves. He even ducked under a hedge, but the stranger still followed him. At last Mr. Brown turned and faced the man. "Why are you following me?" he demanded. "Well, sir, I am going to Mr. Smith's home, and the station agent told me to follow you, since Mr. Smith lives next door to you. Tell me, do you always take this route home?" Often we feel like asking a speaker if he must always take such a roundabout method to reach his main point.

Because we are preaching for a verdict, it is in order occasionally to use an abrupt, unanticipated challenge. At times we can employ material that has "cutting power" as G. K. Chesterton did when he criticized the Christian Social Union at Nottingham for its failure to act. He wrote a verse in which he pointed out that the members of the Union felt it was, of course, their duty to do something; so they sang a lot of hymns "to help the unemployed!"

Eager for our hearers to experience a high hour of dedication to some Christian service to which they have not yet responded, we may recall one of C. T. Studd's poems.

> *Some wish to live within the sound*
> *Of church or chapel bell;*
> *I want to run a rescue shop*
> *Within a yard of hell.*

Certainly today any of us could run a rescue shop, along with Jesus Christ, less than a yard from hell—if we only would.

VI

THE THEMATIC SERMON

Because the thematic sermon can be quite simple in structure, many preachers feel it is the easiest blueprint to follow. The pattern always has one central theme. The subject may be approached from a variety of angles, but the emphasis must be on one idea. The material may be drawn from many sources, but it all converges on the central thought which the minister wishes to underscore.

Indeed, at some time most preachers have selected a verse of Scripture to be used, not merely as the text of the sermon, but also as the subject. "There is a lad here" is a good illustration. This brief verse lends itself admirably for emphasis as text and topic.

I. "There Is a Lad Here"

Anticipating this procedure, consider the possibilities of Andrew's five-word statement: "There is a lad here" (John 6:9). Manifestly an introduction which is both historical and biblical is desirable. Such a beginning gives added meaning to the text, as we describe the situation which caused Jesus to inquire of Philip, "Whence shall we buy bread, that these may eat?" and Philip to reply, "Two hundred pennyworth of bread is not sufficient" (John 6: 5, 7).

Thus, at the outset we remind our congregation of what occurred that day on the hillside. A real problem was posed in feeding so many people. It was then that Andrew said, "There is a lad here. He has five barley loaves and two small fish: but what are they among so many?"

After this introduction the first major point could then be presented, namely, a discussion of the lad who is *now* in our home, in the school, in the church. His environment includes the family, the teachers in his school, those who

75

compose the membership of the church and other social groups of which he is a member. The lad, who has not yet attained maturity, is being influenced by those who associate with him. Because the immediate purpose of the sermon is vitally relevant to the major emphasis, the social, professional, or religious group to whom we address ourselves will determine the material we use. That must always be of interest to the members of the congregation.

It is logical, in the second division of the sermon, to emphasize that the youth is going to become an adult. His environment is, therefore, of tremendous significance. It involves every relationship which this young person sustains.

In the third place, since there is a lad here, and because our influence is so significant for both his present and his future, we are compelled to acknowledge our obligations. Each of us has an inescapable responsibility.

When life is apparently so cheap that we can calmly talk of millions being blown to bits, we are compelled to see the relevancy of this devaluation of human life to the world revolution. When we think of the destruction of what we consider dear, the fact of our responsibility is forced upon us. The possible wholesale slaughter of little children presents the issue as Herod's crime, recorded in Matthew's Gospel (2:16), never could. Although most of us find it difficult to grasp the facts, present world conditions throw a blazing light on these words of Andrew.

Moving to our conclusion, we can point out that, instead of thinking primarily of our responsibility, we will stress the privilege which we are to seize and gladly use. Emphasizing the power of motive, we reaffirm the central theme which is also the text and subject: "There is a lad here."

It is possible, of course, to use this point as a conclusion, making it brief and appealing, as we seek a definite commitment on the part of the congregation. The dedication may be silent and may concern individuals as such; that is, it may be one which each worshiper makes for himself during the singing of the closing hymn or in the prayer of benediction. It may be more specific, following some procedure which has been previously planned by the minister. The technique used for registering certain decisions may include the use of cards available for those who express a willingness to teach in the church school or to enlist in some other program related to the youth.

If the theme has been handled as well as highly trained editorial writers present their columns—which are almost regularly of a thematic nature—the didactic emphasis will be suggested only briefly, if at all.

II. "I Want to Live"

Consider another text quite familiar: "I am come that they might have life, and that they might have it more abundantly" (John 10:10). A related subject will immediately create interest: "I Want to Live!" Jesus' statement confirms every idea worthy of use in handling this theme.

There are, of course, other texts which could well serve as the biblical basis for a similar sermon. What is important to remember, relevant to the thematic sermon, is that the central purpose gains force when it is at the heart of the text. Whatever the sermon is, moreover, it should always reach a climax in some Christian truth. Indeed, *always we are interpreters of God's Word, not presenting our own ideas of life.* This is no less true of the thematic message than it is of the sermon of exposition.

The introduction for a sermon of this pattern may be categorical or life situation. It may be deliberately planned for the purpose of winning a friendly hearing, as we prayerfully anticipate a happy response. Eager for immediate entrée into the minds and hearts of our hearers, we could introduce our subject by saying:

I want to live. But, then, who does not? For although no one is able thoroughly to understand life, we believe that

77

life belongs to us—and that it ought to be good. There are hours when the mighty sweep of its challenge surges over us. Sometimes it is like the exhilaration that comes to a sailor when the salty waves dash across the deck of his ship. He thrills at the thought of matching his strength with the might of the sea.

1. RELIGION MEANS LIFE NOW

Since we plan to emphasize the central theme of this text from various angles, it is neither necessary nor wise to use a long introduction. We move quickly into the first main point, one which may show that religion at its best means life *now*. Underscoring this truth, we readily confess that, in spite of Jesus' assertion that he came to bring life, many still insist that the major purpose of religion is to prepare us to die. Obviously, we quickly add, there is truth in this assertion—enough truth to confuse those who do not reason clearly. Certainly it is hardly necessary to insist that we ought to be ready for death when it comes. But *the primary purpose of Christianity is to prepare us for life*. Life comes *before* death, and some of us believe *after* death. No wonder that when we really find abundant life, we spontaneously exclaim, "I want to live!"

A human interest story would certainly be in order. Indeed, this type of illustration makes an almost universal appeal. A suggestion, relevant to the theme, came to me a few years ago in the course of a conversation I had with Evangeline Booth. Speaking of how life and religion naturally belong together, she told of riding with a London taxi driver who was driving with such speed in the London traffic that there was imminent danger of a collision. Miss Booth vividly described how she leaned over and shouted, "I'm not ready to die!" The taxi driver glanced at her uniform and smiling, exclaimed, "I thought you people were always ready to die." "Well, I'm not!" shouted this devoted Christian with a keen sense of humor. Of course not! Having just been elected head of the Salvation Army, she was eager for a chance to render the finest possible service for under-privileged people everywhere in the world.

A plain statement of theology is thus vital for the thematic sermon. Normally this would be presented in the simplest terms possible. We can remind our congregation, for instance, that we are ready to greet today eagerly only when we believe that Jesus spoke intelligently and accurately when he declared, "I am come that they might have life." For sincere devotees of Christ this means that LIFE, spelled with capital letters, is possible for those who follow him.

Without this assurance we soon reach the conclusion that human existence is senseless. Those who think man is insignificant in our universe may not go to the extreme of Theodore Dreiser, who moaned: "As I see him, the un-utterably infinitesimal individual weaves among the mysteries a floss-like and wholly meaningless course—if course it be. In short, I catch no meaning from all I have seen, and pass quite as I came, confused and dismayed." With such a philosophy, we could scarcely be expected to say with enthusiasm, "I want to live!"

If, moreover, we continue to talk of recovery from grief being easy after a third of our population has been mur-dered—as some men are now suggesting—we can have little idea of what Jesus meant by coming to bring the more abundant life. Instead, we shall be compelled to accept some form of fatalism.

Some have, indeed, discovered the secrets of great religion even when they have been physically handicapped. Recall Helen Keller. Without sight or hearing, "robbed" of what most people think makes human existence desirable, she has demonstrated magnificent living. This achievement is vitally relevant to theology as she makes clear in her testimony: "I cannot imagine myself without religion. I could as easily fancy a living body without a heart. To one who is deaf and blind, the spiritual world offers no difficulty. My mystic world is lovely with trees and clouds and stars and eddying streams I have never 'seen.' I am often conscious of beautiful flowers and birds and laughing children, where to my seeing associates there is nothing."

2. WHEN PURPOSE PROPELS US

In the second major division of the sermon we could suggest what happens when purpose propels us. We begin by pointing out that Christianity means life now because it gives meaning to human existence. Christians have a "reason for life."

We show how a central aim, a goal, a challenging objective, always helps to pull us together. Consider Giotto who sat by the roadside drawing the picture of his sheep on a smooth slate with a stone for a pencil. Then there passed by Cimabue, the leading artist of Florence. He watched Giotto, told him he could be an artist, and invited this talented youth to his studio. After that, all of Giotto's life came together. When that experience is ours, life is new again. We can enthusiastically shout, "I want to live!"

In stressing the essential importance of purpose, we may refer to Sir Henry Jones, who often told his classes that the most pathetic line in Shakespeare is this: "Othello's occupation's gone." Certainly any person misses life when he has no work comparable to his ability. For really to live means to have a high purpose and to move steadily toward its attainment. The "thrill of accomplishment" is ours to the degree we progress toward some goal which helps to pull us together and deepens our desire to reach it.

If, to be sure, our highest aspiration is merely to continue existing in a battered world, we shall neither understand what a great purpose means nor receive the power it can bestow. If we can show, however, that the purpose which continues to propel us must challenge our strength and ability, we may remind our hearers of those who conquered the highest mountain in the world.

In his widely read volume, *The Conquest of Everest*, Sir John Hunt underscores certain phases of this vital truth.

He points out that "the tussle between men and a mountain reaches beyond the scope of mountain climbing in its physical aspects." It is a struggle in which man has been engaged across the years, in attempting to come to terms with the forces of nature. It also speaks of a bond which unites all who have taken part in it. It is no wonder that when a group of students asked Sir John Hunt, "What was the point of climbing Everest?" he gave the answer Mallory had made famous before disappearing in an effort to climb the same mountain. His words still grip us, "Because it's there!"

Consider "the mountain" of a decent world in which to live, "the mountain" of peace among nations, races, and various social groups. What Jesus had in mind when he said we were to pray "Our Father" makes this sermon relevant to life everywhere today.

Certainly any worthy purpose must be vitally related to the immediate present. Recall, for instance, Thornton Wilder's play in which he depicts a character about to die, who asks for the privilege of coming back to earth again to live over one day. "I'll choose a happy day!" she exclaims. But an older and wiser spirit advises, "No! Choose the least important day. . . . It will be important enough!" This friend well knew that time has the touch of eternity. No wonder the terse comment of Dr. Samuel Johnson sometimes stings us, "Time once passed never returns."

Beyond the truth that there is no day which is insignificant, therefore, we see that a worthy aim can be manifest in every experience of life. That means every day. If we miss some challenging objective, even during those days which seem least meaningful, we can be sure we miss *purpose itself.*

3. Purpose for Other People

In the third major division of the sermon it is logical to point out that purpose becomes more significant, as well as more comprehensive, when it includes other people. Those who think it selfish to want to live have not thought too deeply about life. In the first place, they go right on living! Furthermore, they continue to think of their own welfare. Of course, when we are at our best, we want to make life richer and better for other people as well as for ourselves.

Here is the point of departure for the Christian interpretation. For we never become our best selves until we think of other "selves." Woodrow Wilson put it concisely, "The man who gives himself exclusively to the cultivation of his own soul is in danger of becoming a hopeless prig." To which we can add, He is not in danger of losing his religion; he has already abandoned it.

Lord Shaftesbury caught something of the importance of this truth. Only a little while before his death, speaking in Parliament, he confessed, "I hate to think of leaving the world with so much misery in it." He had a real reason for wanting to live. Thousands of children had advantages they could never have known, save for his efforts. He had made life brighter for tens of thousands of working people. He reminds us that the only adequate commentary on Jesus' words, "I am come that ye might have life," is Christ's own life. From Bethlehem to Calvary he was concerned with the welfare of mankind.

We recall the challenge which Wilberforce gave the younger Pitt when he said: "You are the kind of man who ought to be fighting some evil thing. Find some great evil in our national life and give your life to fighting it. . . . I know what it ought to be. Take the slave trade! Find out something about it! Fight it!" Pitt accepted the challenge and turned the idea into action.

The length of this sermon will determine the amount of homiletical material we will use. Perhaps we may wish to refer to what occurred when England was gathering her resources to resist Napoleon. In season and out Wilberforce had been writing, thinking, speaking, working out his plans. Although he was hated as few men have been, he never flinched. Then came a memorable night in the House of

Commons when Wilberforce, now much older, was present but unable to take part in the debate.

Just before "the division" was called, another member of the group arose. A summary of his speech included these statements: "Mr. Chairman, I have been thinking tonight of two heads and of two pillows. A head on a pillow in a distant island is doubtlessly tossing restlessly. It is perhaps because the man who tries to sleep has left a trail of blood all over Europe. I have been thinking also (and here he looked at Wilberforce, who was shading his eyes with his hand) of my honorable friend, the hero of many a long battle who will see the consummation of his life's work. As his head rests upon the pillow he will realize that all about the world, the underprivileged, the suffering, and the downcast will have new hope because of the work he has done. If I could choose, I would rather have the head which rests upon the pillow of Wilberforce than the head which lies upon the pillow of Napoleon."

At once the reserve of that great body of men broke down entirely, and there was wave upon wave of thundering applause.

4. Transforming Purpose

Moving to a fourth major division of the sermon, we show that purpose becomes truly powerful when it brings nobility to character. Worthy objectives include the welfare of others, but they become much more significant when they *transform us.* Jesus was underscoring one facet of this truth when he asked, "Is not the life more than meat, and the body than raiment?" (Matt. 6:25). Luke's Gospel gives the positive response, "The life is more than meat, and the body is more than raiment" (Luke 12:23). Again Jesus declares, "He that findeth his life shall lose it: and he that loseth his life for my sake shall find it" (Matt. 10:39).

The kind of homiletical material relevant for this point is vividly suggested by an incident which occurred on the campus of Emory University.

A few years ago a second-year medical student came into the Alumni office. After a hurried exchange of greetings, he said to the editor of The Alumnus, "Just wanted to tell you how Professor Walker died." "Tell me about it," requested the editor. The student then added, "I don't think you ought to handle Dr. Walker's death with a routine obituary notice. The way he died was the most impressive thing I've seen in the six years I've been at Emory. It's all we've been talking about over in the medical school."

"Tell me about it," the editor requested.

"Okay. You see, Dr. Walker had been sick for two and a half years or so. Hodgkins sarcoma. He'd known for at least six months that he'd never get well. He knew he was slowly dying and so did all of us students, though he never mentioned it and neither did we. We sat there just watching him waste away, but not even that would keep him from his classroom. . . . Why, he taught us a week before he died. . . . He dragged himself up there before us week after week and taught us well, dying a little bit every day. . . .

"We began to realize what we were getting in medical school and what it took to give it to us and how little we were giving. . . . One of the professors said that watching Dr. Walker die the way he did gave him hope that there was enough of the same substance in all men, including himself, to permit them to face death in the same way.

"Here's something else: On Sunday night, the night before he died, Dr. Walker walked into Emory Hospital and told an intern, 'I've come into the hospital to die.' He was gone in less than twenty-four hours. . . ."[1]

Dr. Harry Arthur Walker, Jr., Associate Professor of Pharmacology in Emory's School of Medicine had no power to determine when he should die, but he was able to demonstrate in an unforgettable manner the way to die.

"The whole time (Mrs. Walker) was just as cheerful . . . always friendly and helpful to the students. . . . Dr. Walker showed us how to die," the same student pointed out, "and she's showing us how to accept death!" This man's purpose

---

[1] The Emory Alumnus, December, 1953, p. 5. Used by special permission.

for life transformed him—and doubtless helped others to discover the same power.

If we desire to pinpoint this same truth as it has to do specifically with evangelism, we can refer to George Whitefield who demonstrated a similar passion. "Believe me, I am willing to go to prison and to death for you," he declared. "But I am not willing to go to heaven without you."

When he arrived at Newburyport for the last time, because he was too ill to leave the vessel, they carried him to the parsonage of Old South Church. Toward evening he revived. While he was at supper, crowds began to gather in front of the house. "I am tired," said Whitefield. Taking his lighted candle, he started to bed. But the throng that filled the hall and street, patiently waiting, was too much for him. He paused on the staircase to speak. His voice went on pleading until the candle burned down to the holder.

For the conclusion of a sermon of this pattern, it would be in order to summarize briefly, without any suggestion of haste, employing such ideas as these:

To live to the full is to care for mankind with the undying affection of Jesus Christ. Such love pushes back the horizons of our minds and hearts until we can take in all mankind.

Jesus wanted to live. His prayer in the garden of Gethsemane passionately discloses his longing. He was ready to die *because he had really lived.*

If poetry is preferred to a prose summary, it, too, offers the possibility of a challenge. In "To-Day,"[2] one of her notable poems, Angela Morgan makes this vivid. She challenges us to rise from "despairing knees," fling our "sorrows to the wind," and link our "hope with humankind."

Whatever may be the central truth of the thematic sermon, we are to stay with it from the time we announce the text until the sermon is concluded. If we hold steadfastly to the biblical affirmation we are presenting, we need never lose our way—or our congregation.

---

[2]In *Masterpieces of Religious Verse,* pp. 355-356.

VII

THE COUNSELOR IN THE PULPIT

The Christian minister who learns the art of counseling is equipped to increase the effectiveness of his pastoral work manyfold. Indeed, in a time of anxiety such as ours, no preacher is prepared for his work unless he can, to some degree, aid his people in meeting the fears which constantly beset them. The revolutionary forces, so seriously affecting our world, are nowhere more vividly manifested than in the confused, frustrated minds and hearts of men. Nervous breakdowns are no longer uncommon. It is a paradox that in this day of staggering successes in science, people are succumbing in alarming numbers to nervous disorders. Anxiety assails them on every hand—politically, socially, and personally.

Specialists tell us that every other patient hospitalized is mentally ill. Within the short span of a generation the psychiatrist has, for many people, become the symbol of hope and of salvation.

For us, as Christians, there is a point beyond which most doctors cannot go. This is because there is no real meaning for life apart from our spiritual experience with God. This means the minister has a special and unique place in understanding people and helping them to resolve their fears, obsessions, and anxieties.

Nevertheless, the minister must always be aware that no matter how well he knows the techniques of helping individuals, unless his pulpit messages win the confidence of his hearers, it is not likely that many troubled parishioners will come to his counseling room.

If we are wise, therefore, with discreet sensitivity and with delicate subtlety we will often refer to the deeper needs of individuals. This will make it possible for us to win the response of our parishioners.

I. KNOWLEDGE OF NEED

Of course, our ability to do this is dependent on a number of factors. One is a knowledge of contemporary conditions and an understanding of their influence on us. Two world wars in one generation plus a social revolution have radically changed human relationships in unnumbered ways. During this time, the tempo of life has been speeded up beyond our capacity to adjust to it easily. All this has had a devastating effect on the minds and nerves of people.

What makes this situation even more serious is the fact that national and world-wide peace can never be achieved so long as hosts of persons are engaged in civil war in their own minds and hearts. Only those ministers who are keenly aware of these inward wars can manifest that insight which causes individuals to come to them for consultation and guidance. Our pulpit messages must reveal both moral understanding of our world and a deep appreciation of human need, if we would create confidence on the part of those who need to turn to their pastors for aid.

II. CHARACTERISTICS OF THE CHRISTIAN COUNSELOR

At least to some degree, every well-trained minister is familiar with the personal equipment necessary for counseling. He knows, therefore, that his sermons must disclose a Christian faith that springs from personal experience. Thus, religion, as we present it, will be much more than the accumulated spiritual wisdom and ethical principles which have come down to us across the centuries. Again and again we will emphasize the necessity for faith in the God who is like Christ. Dealing with people who have lost hope, we will discuss various methods by which confidence can be recovered.

We will not merely talk about love that is Christlike; we will seek to manifest sincere friendliness, so that people who hear our sermons may feel religious reality in our messages. They see that our lives are touched with something of that deep concern for human welfare so vividly described by Paul in the thirteenth chapter of First Corinthians. For Christian ministers this sincerity and concern are indispensable. A highly skilled surgeon may have many patients primarily because of his medical knowledge and his scientific efficiency. As counselors, however, our effectiveness can be demonstrated only to the degree that our Christian personalities win the response of our parishioners.

This gracious spirit is much more than a kindly attitude. It goes beyond, and is far deeper than, the art of winning friends and influencing people. It has to do with genuine regard for the total well-being of others. It is affection, sincere and intelligent. It faces toward, and reflects, the devotion demonstrated in the life and death of Christ.

When our parishioners believe that we know the art of listening with understanding, they will come to us with confidence. They may not be sure that we can diagnose their mental confusion or accurately analyze their spiritual ills, but they will at least be convinced that our attitude will make us sympathetic listeners.

Certainly our messages will include references which disclose knowledge of both personal and social psychology. Our familiarity with these subjects does not become an academic display of scholarship. Rather, our training will be manifested in insights, references, and illustrations that are necessary for well-planned sermons.

So, too, we subtly suggest that we have some knowledge of both the indispensable importance and limitations of uncommon common sense in dealing with those who are disturbed mentally and emotionally. As Theodor Reik has pointed out: "There are certain problems that can be solved by common sense and logic . . . but they are not the most important problems that face the psychoanalist."[1] Nor are they the most perplexing problems that face the preacher

[1] *Listening with the Third Ear* (Farrar Straus and Co.), p. 192.

who becomes a counselor. The really vital issues require spiritual sensitivity which we can cultivate only when we rid ourselves of prejudice and immaturity by developing concern for all God's children.

1. INTEGRATION OF THE INDIVIDUAL

Our ultimate goal is, of course, the complete integration of our parishioners as well as of ourselves. Often, however, it is necessary to seek this wholeness by means of ascending levels. This method requires skill, for it means encouraging people by helping them to lesser attainments without suggesting moral or spiritual compromise. In various ways we promise hope to those who despair. Some decisions are immediately necessary. Often, however, there are many steps in the journey to complete integration, or salvation. The intelligent preacher takes into consideration various levels of mental, ethical, and spiritual development. John Wesley must have been thinking of this when he discussed "The repentance of believers."

Obviously, the counselor must be unshockable. Therefore, we never speak of our being *surprised, disappointed, discouraged, shocked,* or *disgusted.* These terms and the attitudes they disclose create fear on the part of those who come to us because they are troubled. Furthermore, when we reveal—either publicly or privately—that we are shocked or surprised, we indicate that we lack the objectivity necessary for diagnosis.

This requisite of mental and emotional maturity will be manifested not merely in our pulpit messages, but by those attitudes which clearly indicate our awareness that we, too, are in need of God's forgiveness and grace, along with those who have come to church or the counseling room for help. Realizing that we can never be pharisaical if we are effective counselors, we cultivate humility and mental and spiritual rapport with our people by keeping in mind the Christian standard: "Be ye perfect as your Father . . . is perfect" (Matt. 5:48).

2. Emotional Stability

Emotional stability is indispensable for the minister who has an earnest desire to speak to the deepest needs of people as they worship in the sanctuary. Nervousness robs us of calm and objectivity and thus prevents us from dealing with people effectively.

A recent novel presents this idea dramatically. A surgeon finds it necessary to operate on a man whom he had severely wounded in a duel. The operation required calm nerves. Manifestly, under such circumstances, any doctor would find it advantageous to abandon hatred, which unnerves those who succumb to it. This particular operation was successful because a man dismissed his anger and worked as a skillful surgeon.

Certainly, our judgments cannot be clear as long as we are swayed by emotional disturbances which are the result of ill will, acknowledged or unconfessed. "Forgive us our trespasses as we forgive those who trespass against us," and "I say unto you that you are to forgive seventy times seven" are vivid reminders of an essential Christian attitude.

Any preacher who is successful with the sermon of counseling must cultivate confidence on the part of his parishioners and counselees by never betraying them. He also demonstrates this basic rule by refusing to use illustrations that would betray the trust of those who come for help. A few years ago a minister, who forgot how important this is, wrote a book in which he disclosed the secrets of certain parishioners. It was necessary for him to leave the section of the state in which he had formerly rendered effective service. This result was surely to be anticipated.

Some time ago a friend stressed the importance of never violating the confidence of a parishioner. It had been impossible to talk frankly with a certain pastor, he declared. The reason? In his sermons that minister often related experiences of those who had conferred with him during the week—and frequently in minute detail.

It should be clear to all who preach that any personal

illustrations must be set in the pattern of generalizations, thus making it impossible for worshipers to recognize those individuals related to the incident. This is good sense as well as Christian appreciation of others.

3. The Use and Power of Prayer

Certainly, the Christian counselor is a man of prayer. He is constantly learning *how* to pray. Even more vital, he understands the importance of preparing himself for each message with prayer. Since he cannot stand in the pulpit and announce, "I am a man of prayer," the minister adopts techniques which create trust on the part of his congregation. His attitude and spirit will say, "You can come to me in confidence because I have gone to God in prayer." Thus our sermons disclose an awareness of God that causes our parishioners to feel that each message is sacramental.

4. Content Cultivates Confidence

What we preach should also create trust as it promises help. Although many of our people in mental perplexity and spiritual confusion may not readily confess it, they are seeking *reality*. We can meet their needs as we ourselves become aware of the Spirit of God. Thus we identify ourselves with the Highest and in our pulpit ministry manifest the ability to transcend low motives. Serenity of mind, resulting from a deep desire for fellowship with God, must be constantly cultivated by those who anticipate becoming counselors.

Our philosophy and theology will, of course, make our hearers conscious of the power of the Divine Spirit. Although some materialistic psychiatrists may aid people temporarily, there are critical issues all of us face which they can never handle. Obviously they do not know what to do with death. The Christian minister is able to speak to this personal crisis from the authority of the Scriptures, by interpreting the life of Christ, and with the reinforcement of his own inner assurance. Always remembering that

91

the one reason for the sermon of counseling is to lead individuals to Christ and leave them with him, each of us will choose the material which aids us in accomplishing this purpose.

Thus do we stress mental quietude and spiritual peace. Unreasonable hurry and overcrowded schedules result in the loss of our souls. Those who do not agree with much that Bertrand Russell has said are, nevertheless, arrested by his assertion that we are now suffering not from a decay of theological belief but from a loss of solitude.[2] Thus by means of various techniques and a variety of illustrations, we teach our people "to *relax, realize,* and *resolve*."[3]

III. EMPHASIZING SELF-KNOWLEDGE

Because it is a requisite for spiritual understanding, all possible self-knowledge is a necessary preparation for counseling experiences. No matter what other resources or talents we possess, if we lack self-understanding and intellectual poise, we are incapable of facing life steadily and seeing it whole. Paul understood this when he exhorted, "Examine yourselves, whether ye be in the faith" (II Cor. 13:5). This is not morbid introspection; it is needed information and a wholesome analysis of ourselves.

Our sermons should make it easier for people to gain the same knowledge of themselves. By depicting the dangers of daydreaming, for instance, we show that those who indulge in fantasies needlessly waste their energies. They imagine what they want to become when they should be using their resources in accomplishing their professed purposes.

We can also depict how most alibis reveal conscious or unconscious failure. Confessing our faults is much more difficult than offering excuses for them. Too many of us are like the man who, when asked if he ever gave serious

---

[2]*Life Victorious,* Joseph Fort Newton (Fleming H. Revell, New York), p. 64.
[3]*Ibid.,* p. 65.

thought to the mistakes he made, answered too glibly that such contemplation of his shortcomings invariably caused him to fall asleep.

In some sermon that provokes self-knowledge we will discuss the almost universal desire for attention and the subconscious longing for power. Literally millions try to do whatever will make others notice them and applaud their acts. Lincoln once declared that if a certain general had known what a big funeral he was to have, he would have died much earlier!

The well-trained Christian minister also deals with *over-assertion* and *under-assertion*. The clerk who "explodes" at the baseball park is indulging in the former. So is the person who shouts into the telephone. All such acts are usually the result of an inferiority complex.

Under-assertion is just as serious a mistake. Dickens has a character, Uriah Heap, whose very name has been associated with the art of "glorifying one's inferiority in order to use it as a foil to win what one deeply desires." We need to learn what tragedy results from such twists in the mind.

. *Infantile regression* is such a common fault that we have an over-abundance of material which forcefully reveals how immature most of us are. So many scholars have written in this field that ministers can follow the principles without unnecessary strain, although often it is with embarrassment!

So, too, *sensation* can be presented as one of the compensations which thousands of young people seek by means of misconduct, crime, and uninhibited emotional outbursts. They indulge in abnormal excitements because they are not "grown." They have not matured.

Certainly it is plain that the speed of modern life—part of our social revolution—often robs us of deep understanding of life and of ourselves. Instead of our having no need of quietude, of which Jesus spoke so often, the rush of life, added to the dangers of mass destruction, makes this experience far more necessary than most people have ever imagined.

93

Only as we know ourselves will we be able to manage our moods or deal effectively with any serious difficulty that concerns our personal relationships. Self-knowledge, however, is not easily gained. Shakespeare had this in mind when he made Antonio say:

> In soothe I know not why I am so sad:
> It wearies me; you say it wearies you;
> But how I caught it, found it, or came by it,
> What stuff 'tis made of, whereof it is born,
> I am to learn.[4]

There is some encouragement in recalling, as Dr. W. L. Northridge has reminded us, that only the superficial or the insane escape mental depression. The saints, the mystics, the dedicated scholars have to face dark hours. Professor John Baillie has etched this on our minds by giving rather personal facts with regard to his brother, Donald Baillie, a saintly scholar.[5]

IV. Teaching How to Gain Peace of Soul

Of course, there is never any permanent peace without spiritual poise. Yet, because human nature is so complex, before we are aware of what is happening many of us become divided personalities. This is the result of failing to follow the direction of enlightened moral judgment.

Actually we are such complex persons that there can be no ultimate solution for our problems until we attain harmony between the subconscious and the conscious. Thus Jesus spoke with scientific accuracy when he insisted that we must be born again. The least he meant was that our subconscious must be in tune with the will of God, if we are ever able happily and spontaneously to respond to the divine call. Because "the soul is a wide country," as Schniz-

---

[4]*The Merchant of Venice,* Act I, Scene 1, lines 1-5.
[5]*Disorders of the Emotional and Spiritual Life* (Channel Press, 1961), p. 6.

ler[6] says, we can range far with our minds. Remembering that patterns of thought can project themselves into action, we become exceedingly careful in forming mental habits. "As [a man] thinketh in his heart, so is he" (Prov. 23:7). Sensing the serious implications of this, Paul enumerated the finest thoughts possible for any human being, as he urged his friends in Philippi: "Think on these things" (Phil. 4:8).

By dealing with universal dangers and difficulties, we shall not merely be appealing to worshipers in our congregation; we shall also be making it easier for others to come for conference.

We may not leave our hearers "in stitches" as does the comedian of stage and pulpit, but we can show them the way to the Cross, where they can be saved from sin, irresponsibility, and mass culture with its entangling alliances. We can show that the success of science means ultimate failure, unless we "succeed" with God as we are used by him in making the world a brotherhood.

V. Release from Fear

One of the personal problems with which we must constantly deal is fear. It is so widespread that some have declared it is "an instinctive emotion." There are times it does seem almost innate. Paradoxical as it seems, fear can make for efficiency. The surgeon who is without fear is hardly equipped for delicate and critical operations. Only the airplane pilot who has fear of failing to follow the directions from the tower assures safety for his passengers. When Angelo Patri says, "Education consists in being afraid at the right time," he underscores the same truth. E. E. Marett, the English scientist, summarizes the basic principle: "The function of fear is to induce a needful caution."

Writing of his experience in the trenches during World

---

[6] *Listening with the Third Ear,* Theodor Reik (Farrar Straus and Co.), p. 173.

War I, Herbert A. Gray declares that he met only two kinds of men: "Those who conquered fear and went on with their work and those who were conquered by fear. I met none who did not know fear."[7]

When the preacher distinguishes between fear that paralyzes and fear that instructs, he begins to move up to a high level. Thus he is able not merely to depict the difference between anxiety and fear, but also to explain why "the fear of the Lord"—which involves awe and reverence—"is the beginning of wisdom."

C. J. Hambro, Norwegian delegate to the League of Nations, must have been thinking of this when he summarized the failure of the League in these cryptic and cutting words: "In Geneva we have every fear but the fear of God." This statement helps us see how intricately involved are personal disintegration and international confusion. Fear of doing wrong may, indeed, force us into the path of right. Facing a guilty conscience should lead us ultimately to Christian salvation.

With this in mind, we help make religion real by using texts like Luke 2:10: "Fear not; for behold I bring you good tidings of great joy." Other relevant biblical material which always thrills, excites, and challenges would include: "Fear not; I am the first and last: I am he that liveth, and was dead; and, behold, I am alive for evermore; . . . and have the keys of hell and of death" (Rev. 1:17-18). These words came to a man when dread of the Roman Empire was so pronounced that he felt compelled to use allegorical terms in describing the conquerors of his country.

Whatever the major emphasis of the sermon of counseling, there is a text for it. As one interprets many biblical statements, he will discuss contemporary crises for the understanding of which truth expressed by the writer is exactly pertinent. There will be times, of course, when most of the sermon will deal with dangers of today. Even so, the truth

[7]*The Secret of Inward Peace* (Macmillan Company), p. 43.

expressed by God's Word is of supreme importance. For man's needs are essentially the same across the centuries. Present-day conditions only depict these in a new setting. We are not merely restless until we find God; we are hopeless without him.

When we see life steadily and whole, we lift our eyes to the eternal hills whence comes our help. Round our restlessness does flow his rest. We learn that Christ spoke with authority when he said, "If a man love me, he will keep my words: and my Father will love him and we will come unto him and make our abode with him" (John 14:23).

Eventually we show that cure for fears goes beyond managing them. Many of us are beginning to see this because of the alarm with regard to the hydrogen bomb. Indeed, the Christian learns he can master this enemy when he himself is mastered by the Master.

Thus faith is a force that destroys fear and the sense of futility.

> *Courage is armour*
> *A blind man wears,*
> *The calloused scar*
> *Of outlived despairs.*
> *Courage is Fear*
> *That has said its prayers.*[8]

So we tell our people of those who have accepted God's power. Hear two of their confident affirmations: "Cast thy burden on the Lord"; "God is our refuge and strength" (Pss. 55:22; 46:1). Eventually we guide them to Christ, whose invitation is all-inclusive: "Come unto me, all ye that labor and are heavy laden, and I will give you rest" (Matt. 11:28).

In a way men have never known, we now are forced to deal with the fear of destruction of our property and of our lives. It is imperative that we help people to understand why Paul was able to declare that whether we live

---

[8]"Courage," Karle Wilson Baker, from *The Burning Bush* (Yale University Press).

or die, we are in the hands of God. As Christian ministers our responsibility, as well as our privilege, is that of making frightened people see that Paul was not penning a peroration, but was testifying with regard to his assurance of triumph when he exclaimed, "O death, where is thy sting?" (I Cor. 15:55).

Fortunately many followers of Christ have learned this truth. Consider those millions who a few years ago were facing death at the hands of the Nazis. Many of them learned how to keep calm and confident. It is fitting that a book which presents numerous letters some of these wrote to friends and members of their families should be titled, *Dying We Live*.[9]

VI. CHRIST AND OUR CONFESSION

Thus we encourage our hearers to practice prayerful catharsis by holding up their fears, anxieties, and sins not simply for their own understanding, but for divine examination. Only a power greater than our own can manage our moods and give us an inner sense of security. Self-deception, therefore, is a luxury we cannot afford. It gives us a false sense of security.

We speak to the deepest needs of all our hearers when we tell them that confession of sin means going much farther than mere verbal catharsis. It is far more than simply talking things out. The conviction of sin and wrongdoing, followed by repentance and a desire to lead a better life, makes it possible for us to seek divine forgiveness and cleansing power.

Becoming aware of our mistakes, foibles, and sins, we begin to see the positive advantages of confession. *Scarlet Letter* is an illustration of homiletical material which discloses the terrific power of unconfessed sin and suggests the only way of relief and release. This novel emphasizes the deeper meaning of Eliot's penetrating lines:

*Fontana Books, London, 1958.

Where does one go from a world of insanity?
Somewhere on the other side of despair.

. . . .

I must follow the bright angels.[10]

By way of encouraging our people, we refer to Christian leaders who, disturbed by fear, have found it necessary and rewarding to confess their weakness. Consider Hugh Latimer, who suffered martyrdom in 1555. Once he exclaimed: "Pray for me! Sometimes I am so afraid I could creep into a mouse hole. So, God cometh and goeth. Pray for me, I beg you." In spite of the fact that he was courageous enough to face death at the stake, Latimer knew times of fright and spiritual confusion.

The Source of strength, to whom he turned, is still available. "Underneath are the everlasting arms" (Deut. 33:27). "God hath not given us the spirit of fear; but of power, and of love, and of a sound mind" (II Tim. 1:7).

VII. FORGIVENESS AND REALITY

The forgiveness of sins and the receiving of strength for life belong together. They are both gracious gifts of God. True absolution is in his divine pardon. Witnessing its cost on Calvary, we never minimize the terror of running athwart the Divine Will. Hence, we explain that our greatest difficulty is not with material, economic, or even international problems. Rather it has to do with our wills. Giving ourselves to God leads us to thrilling truths such as G. A. Studdert Kennedy had in mind when he declared that joy is a gift which God is bestowing upon those who "strive with Him."

VIII. CHRISTIAN CONQUEST

But we must do just that. Although there are ample resources of strength available for every individual who deep-

---

[10]Jarrett-Kerr, Martin, *Our Trespasses* (SCM Press), p. 41.

ly desires them, yet they are not ours until we accept them. For this reason we teach our parishioners practical techniques for discovering power for life and making it intimately real. We spell out why William E. Hocking is right when he declared that only the highest kind of religion "can create the unpurchasable." We, therefore, never forget Christ's words: "Be ye perfect as your Father . . . in heaven is perfect" (Matt. 5:48).

Siegmund Schultze, a German refugee from Hitler, demonstrates how this rapport with God's purposes can bring stability and moral strength. He was able to talk about Hitler without becoming emotionally upset because he was in contact with the Power of the universe. A friend declared that Schultze "seemed to be listening to the tick of an astronomical clock, inaudible to the ears of the dictator."

"There is a God," said Siegmund Schultze with unshaken confidence. "I can wait."[11] We and our parishioners must gain confidence like this, in these days when it seems that our world may be blown into a million smithereens.

IX. God's Greatness Gives Hope

The preacher, therefore, who makes religion practical for the present-day congregation will interpret God's omnipresence as meaning that God's power and strength are available everywhere. God has been our help in ages past, and he will be our hope for all the years to come. While we are building bomb shelters to escape the fall-out, Christianity reminds us that God is "our shelter from the stormy blast and our eternal home"!

Hence, all our public messages cultivate aspiration and provoke desire for dedication. Having established rapport with our people, we are able through counseling to offer them strength, unity, and integration for daily living. In public worship and private conference they come to understand that *God is capable of doing everything that ought to be done and that he is our Friend.*

---

[11] Alan Hunter, in *White Corpuscles in Europe.*

VIII

THEOLOGY THAT THRILLS

As strange as it now seems, between World War I and World War II many church leaders did not consider theology important. Then came the dropping of two A-Bombs on Japanese cities. A growing understanding of what this newly discovered power means has shocked most of us out of our complacency. No longer does anyone who is considered a discerning devotee of religion laugh at theology. Intelligent churchmen have come to realize that our hope is in God, not in unredeemed man.

The Deity, moreover, who is capable of helping us must be able to do what we cannot do for ourselves. If we are to cultivate confidence for tomorrow, we must come to believe that His attitude *toward* us, as well as his concern *for* us, is Christlike. This means that every clergyman who desires to become an effective shepherd of souls must be able to show that theology is vital and essential. This necessitates discussing dependable truth in such a way that it provokes the eager response of those who worship.

I. When Life Becomes Thrilling

Of the many scriptural references which present theology that thrills, here is one particularly appealing: "Fear not, little flock; for it is your Father's good pleasure to give you the kingdom" (Luke 12:32). Obviously the introduction of a sermon based on this affirmation of Jesus should immediately arrest attention and, at the same time, promise that the discussion will hold the interest of the congregation. With this in mind, consider the wisdom of a candid confession of the difficulty of faith. The preacher could begin in this way:

This morning we shall discuss the subject: *When Life Becomes Thrilling*. It sounds unreasonable, almost superficial, does it not? Certainly the idea does not seem to be relevant to life as we now know it. Most of us would not consider asking for thrills. We would happily settle for freedom from fear. But Jesus promises much more. He meets us where we are, perplexed and despondent, and offers drama and excitement. "Fear not little flock," he confidently exclaims, "for it is your Father's good pleasure to give you the kingdom."

If we sustain the interest of those who are wrestling with the disturbing problems of life, we will have to meet them where they are. We will readily admit that many people have found it difficult to accept our text's affirmation at its face value. Gamaliel Bradford comes to mind. In *Life and I* wistfully, if somewhat cynically, he writes of his doubts. With apparent irreverence, he suggests that, even though God lacked some desirable virtues, it would be preferable that we have some deity rather than none at all.

Thomas Hardy also struggled with doubts concerning God. He made one of his characters say that even if there were a God, he could not possibly be good. This fictional character declares that if there is a being in charge of the world, he must be one who takes delight in making people suffer.

If this seems too strong a presentation of the disturbing doubts of perplexed minds, it is at least possible to quote the section of Matthew Arnold's *Dover Beach* in which the author insists that the world has "neither joy, nor life, nor light." On this dark plane, we are swept with "alarms of struggle" and distracted by confusion everywhere. We are where ignorant armies clash by night.

Today the doubts suggested by these individuals seem even more justified than they were in former years. The conditions which confuse minds, already troubled, are retold and dramatically presented day after day in our newspapers. We have to face them with our people.

We may point out that the intellectually brilliant who doubt God listen to references of faith in his purpose and then respond with a Mona Lisa smile. The cynical answer our appeal with brittle laughter. The plain man who wishes he could believe in a divine plan, but feels he cannot, smiles sadly when some friend speaks of a dependable purpose for the universe. At our best, however, all of us know that blessedness is impossible without a genuine and sincere trust in God.

Having admitted the many difficulties of believing in a good God, we reaffirm the statement of Jesus which is our text. As always, the Bible is our base, and the affirmation of Christ is the word we speak.

Whatever the precise language we may use, it is in order to indicate our first major point: *A Divine Plan*. "It is your Father's good pleasure to give you the kingdom." Using the element of surprise, we may employ the technique of deliberately not urging anyone to believe that there is a divine plan. Rather, we dare them to consider what it would mean *if* they could believe that there is a God and that he has a plan for his world. Life would truly become thrilling!

In the second place we may suggest the possibility of believing that God has a purpose for each individual. "It is your Father's pleasure to give *you* the kingdom." Of course it is much more difficult to accept this specific idea as a fact than to give credence to a general plan for the world. If, however, we *act* as if it were true, life does become exciting, dramatic, thrilling.

In the third place, Jesus uses the verb *give* when he explains what God purposes to do. Thus we can point out that there is *power* for each of us to fulfill God's purpose for us. If we do not believe that there are adequate resources for us, accepting the idea that there is a worthy purpose for us would not help us. We would still face frustration and, ultimately, a sense of defeat. To know we ought to live grandly when we have no ability to do so inevitably results in distress and often in a divided person.

103

We can, however, point to many who have accepted divine power for life. Paul and Luther, Athanasius and John Knox, Martin Niemöller and Dietrich Bonhoeffer are names that remind us there is strength adequate to meet crises. Recalling numbers who have been endowed with the ability to execute the divine plan for their lives, we use the names of some who have faced contemporary crises, who know the meaning of the revolution in which we find ourselves.

In the fourth place, we may emphasize the meaning of *personal fellowship*. If we believe what Jesus is saying, namely, that not merely does God have a plan for us and power to help us fulfill this objective, but also that he offers us his personal comradeship, life truly does become exciting. We confidently affirm that we can trust Christ when we recall his reassuring statement that if we keep his words, God will come and abide with us (John 14:23). This is much more than a promise; it is a fact that thousands have experienced for themselves.

II. A Faith That Sings

Another text which suggests the appealing power of theology is in II Timothy 1:12: "I know whom I have believed, and am persuaded that he is able to keep that which I have committed unto him against that day." The writer obviously believes there is a faith that sings. He reminds us of another record: "When they had sung an hymn, they went out into the mount of Olives"[1] (Matt. 26:30).

Whatever we may suggest as the background of either affirmation or trust, it will deal vitally with the idea of faith for all of life. With respect to the statement in Second Timothy, it will be fairly easy in an introduction to point out that belief of some kind is inescapable. We can also effectively employ the element of the unexpected. With this in mind, the minister may say:

---

[1] For additional material, see the author's *Religion That Is Eternal* (Macmillan Co., New York, 1960).

I believe. You believe. We may not believe the same thing, or in the same cause, but each has some kind of faith, even if it is one that doubts! Every person has some creed, for no one can avoid believing something.

It is true that the term *creed* has become distasteful to many individuals. They insist that they cannot accept any specific affirmation of religious faith. Cynicism concerning religion has created widespread doubt. Some criticisms, to be sure, may be justified. Certainly, creeds have been abused by some ardent defenders of faith as well as by others who denounce religion.

Even so, it is not possible to abandon belief. All of us exercise some faith. It is a question of *what* we believe. The most irreligious person believes something. It is his mental attitude that determines his doubts. When we harshly deny the reality of religion, we are describing our faith.

We may believe the world has no religious meaning whatever. This is our privilege. When, however, we sneer at Christianity, we are expressing our creed. To assert that the only possible faith is a lack of faith, that the most optimistic facts serve to justify only a dismal, unrelenting pessimism, is to "recite" our creed with clarity and force. It is that everything will finally go into total eclipse. The night of despair is just ahead.

1. TRUST IN GOD

We may want immediately to consider the phrase, "Whom I have believed." God must be real if we are to have a faith that brings zest for life. In the first main division of the sermon, we can show how relevant this faith in God's existence is to vital religion. We tell our hearers that if we are to experience any real blessedness, it will be because we believe in a Supreme Being—One whose intelligence and power are adequate to deal with the universe.

To believe in God like this does not necessitate our hurling arguments at those who disagree with us. We do not engage in debate for the purpose of battering our way into unbelieving minds. Such would only disclose some secret doubt. On the other hand, we do not stress romantic and superficial reasons for God's existence. These would not help any person who is seriously troubled in his effort to "see life steadily and see it whole." We are eager to help our parishioners find their way through a maze of doubts to a reasonable belief in a Supreme Being who is worthy of worship. We must make faith relevant to all life. Such faith starts a lyric that rings with melody through difficult and dangerous days.

Consider Lisa Goertz, a Jewess in Nazi Germany, who lost husband, son, and daughter. Able to secure passage for England, she traveled "with my hand gripping the hand of Christ." Leaving the country in which she had been born and had "spent so many happy years before the cruel days of persecution," she committed her way, her future, and herself to the God she had seen in Christ.[2]

We readily confess, of course, that such confidence, far from being widely accepted, is too exacting for most people. Its demands are too heavy. As a result, many capitulate to pessimism. C. E. Ayers once declared that we must become evangelists of skepticism. Many who cannot believe the world has spiritual meaning do not go so far as Joseph Wood Krutch, who insists that things are finally unintelligible and that rational principles exist only with ourselves. Nothing in the world, he declares, corresponds to reasonable thinking.

A popular attitude, accepted by many people, is that of simply ignoring God. They recite their creeds in daily conversations, social affairs, drama. Consider the play, *Street Scene*. Love, romance, sordid poverty, avarice, adultery, murder—all are there; just about everything except worship and religion! *You're in the Army, Mr. Jones, Arsenic and Old Lace, Cat on a Hot Tin Roof*, and *Irma La Douce* are a few of many well-known plays that express no need for God, or, indeed, of any religion. They are symbols of the emptiness in which multitudes live.

In view of these facts, it is challenging to hear Robert A. Millikan declare that, from his point of view, the most

---

[2] *I Stepped into Freedom* (Lutterworth Press, London), p. 33.

important thing in our world is confident faith in "the reality of moral and spiritual values." The weal or woe of our race depends, he insists, not upon belief in the possibilities of scientific progress, but upon our faith in the worth of the "Unseen." It was because we lost belief in the great spiritual values that war came. If we do not find a way "to regain and to strengthen" this belief, "science is of no value."

As we confess that this is strong language for a scientist, we remind our hearers that it has to do with the practical character of belief in God. This faith makes all the difference in the world between mere existence and life—vibrant, throbbing, radiant life. Such faith can "split the sky in two" and "let the face of God shine through." Even though Edna St. Vincent Millay later lost this faith, she once vividly portrayed what it could mean.

It is even more important to remember that our doubts do not dismiss God from his universe. When we resign in despair, God still pursues his divine purposes. He speaks when we are silent. When we quit, he continues to work. When we doubt that he reigns, he continues to rule. We can never bomb him off his throne!

2. BELIEF IN CHRIST

In the second division of the sermon, if the mood of the congregation and the atmosphere of the service permit, the preacher may speak quite personally. With reverence and proper restraint, he may add:

I believe more. I believe in Jesus Christ. I do not simply mean that I think there was a man named Jesus who lived nineteen centuries ago. It is true that some people have doubted that Jesus actually lived. However, the more critically we study the records, writes Professor C. H. Dodd, the more certain we are of a real Person in history.

But Jesus is no ordinary individual. He is many sided and often perplexing, since he is "too great to be reduced to any common type." It is unmistakably plain that in Christ we have an individual, "strongly defined" in his character and purpose, who challenges us by "a unique outlook on life." Those who believe this agree with Browning when he declares in the "Epilogue" to his *Dramatis Personae*:

> *That one Face, far from vanish, rather grows,*
> *Or decomposes but to recompose.*

If the mood of the worshipers makes it possible, the preacher can reason kindly, but insistently, as he points out that he believes the Man Jesus Christ sustained some vital relationship to the heart of the universe. If the universe produced him—and it did—we must remember that "it" cannot produce anything finer or better than "it" is. Christ does offer an explanation for all the worlds there are. If we can believe this, we do have a song in our hearts.

But there is no substitute for faith, and it is deeply moving to note how many brilliant non-Christian thinkers have unconsciously suggested this. Consider Martin Heidegger, when he claims that anxiety discloses that man is thrust "into a hostile world" and he is not "at home" here. As Murdo Macdonald wisely comments: "This analysis touches the very threshold of religion. . . . We are permanently anxious in this world, because, in the language of the New Testament, we are 'strangers and pilgrims' here" (I Pet. 2:11).[3]

Again interpreting our text from II Timothy 1:12, we may challenge our hearers with the fact that Christ offers hope that we can be better than we are. Here *is* a creed that sings! It is this that excites us when we recall Jesus' declaration: "He who has seen me has seen the Father." Jesus makes the idea of God so reasonable and so persuasively appealing that those who dare to act on it finally learn that this Deity is the only One they can worship.

But there is more. Whatever we may say about much of the theology relative to the Cross, there is at least some-

[3]*The Need to Believe* (Fontana Books, Hodder and Stoughton, London, 1960).

thing about Calvary which finds us. The Cross deeply moves us. This is because the cross of Christ speaks of the care God has for men. It also suggests what men can become. Part of this John Oxenham must have had in mind when he wrote, "Not what I do believe, but Whom!"

Concluding this main point, quietly but positively we declare our belief in Jesus' way of life. We have never discovered any character finer or more worthy of the devotion of humanity than is Christ. When we think clearly in our best hours, he makes life reasonable for us.

3. BELIEF IN MAN

The minister who is discerning will make it plain that only as we believe in God and Christ can we have Christian confidence in man. Since Jesus is the noblest person the world has ever known, he shows us why we can hope for ourselves.

Relevant to this, it is more than strange that although many critics once bitterly condemned Christianity for teaching that we should confess our weaknesses, now some writers insist that man has no real worth, certainly none that will guarantee his continuing beyond death. None of us, they declare, has any abiding value.

Actually, however, any affirmation of faith which magnifies God as Christ knew him, leads us to rejoice that we believe in man, not because of his amazing scientific discoveries, but because of what he can become in Christian character.

Brother Lawrence, noted for his widely read book, *The Practice of the Presence of God*, gives clear directions even when he uses homely language. He tells us that on those occasions when he was challenged to practice some Christian virtue, he would reverently seek God's help, saying, "Lord, I cannot do this unless Thou enablest me." Then, he adds, he received more than adequate strength. So, when he failed in some "duty," he readily admitted his fault, as he confessed to God: "I shall never do otherwise if You leave me to myself; 'tis You must hinder my falling and mend whatever is amiss."

Here we may remind our hearers that the word "king" comes from *kon-ning*, or *can-ning*, the man who is able. It is the power of God that makes one kingly. Hear Paul: "I have strength for anything through him who gives me power" (Philippians 4:13, NEB).

This is the testimony of thousands who have faced the crises of contemporary conditions without succumbing to compromise or collapsing. Recall the price Carl Friedrich Goerdeler, mayor of Leipzig, had to pay for his activity in the German resistance, when Hitler came into power. Condemned to death, he wrote from his prison cell: "Have we not erred in calling upon the aid of God for national purposes? . . . Christ . . . did not teach love for one's fellow countryman, but for one's neighbor. . . . We can only beg God . . . to give ascendancy to the apostles of reconciliation."

Using even more virile language, Hermann Lange wrote from his prison cell at Hamburg on July 11, 1943: "Personally I am perfectly calm, facing steadfastly what is to come. When one has really achieved complete surrender to the will of God, there is a marvelous feeling of peace and a sense of absolute security. . . .The gift we . . . receive is so unimaginably great that all human joys pale beside it."[4]

Of course it takes skill to lift this idea to the highest possible spiritual level. Nevertheless, it is possible to emphasize that Christ believed, not in the superiority of physical strength, but in the might of the meek. And now, in a day of nuclear warfare, we see more clearly than ever before that concern for others is not merely an ideal, but the only practical way we can live. And it will require far more courage to keep the world at peace, living as one family, than we have yet demonstrated.

---

[4] *Dying We Live*, translated by Reinhard C. Kuhn (Fontana Books, London), pp. 87, 88.

4. God and Tomorrow

It is because we can believe in God and in man—either his inherent or his potential worth—that we can proclaim confidence for tomorrow. We can make the exciting truth vivid by emphasizing that Christianity not merely has a future, but confidently, even exultantly, *sings* of that future. "When they had sung an hymn, they went out into the mount of Olives." Facing the cross, Jesus and his friends *sang*.

As we consider our world, apparently ready to destroy itself, the text becomes more relevant. Indeed, some of us may have to learn how to sing in a fall-out shelter—if we are able to sing at all.

When we can say, "I know whom I have believed," the present tense gains extra force, because Jesus himself emphasized it. Hear him: "He that heareth my word, and believeth on him that sent me, hath everlasting life" (John 5:24). The quality of life is of supreme importance. Heaven begins when *we* begin with a heavenly experience. Its continuance is a reality because we ourselves can continue with God.

Although, as is normally true, various conclusions to this sermon are possible, one of the most satisfactory may be a very brief summary reference to the zestful and songful nature of our faith. Here is a faith that really works. It is practical and practicable. When it is *our* testimony, *we* can say: "I know whom I have believed."

Vividly presenting what confidence in the Christian God can do for us, without dogmatically demanding that others accept the truth, gives us a message that will appeal to many troubled people.

To be effective this sermon requires both skill and art. In the revolutionary days in which most of us will live and die, it also demands the regard for others of which Paul was thinking when he said: "Love is never boastful, nor conceited, nor rude. . . . Love is patient" (I Cor. 13:5, 4, NEB).

111

IX

RELIGION BECOMES REASONABLE

Religion at its best has always appealed to reason. The Old Testament prophets underscore this again and again. "Let us reason together" is not merely the exhortation of Isaiah (1:18); it is the spirit of every outstanding messenger of God. When we enter the New Testament, this fact is even more sharply presented. Numerous passages emphasize its significance. "Three Sabbath days Paul reasoned with them" is the record of Acts 17:2. Of the same herald of the Christian gospel it is written: "He reasoned in the synagogue every Sabbath, and persuaded the Jews and Greeks" (Acts 18:4). Again we read: "Godliness is profitable unto all things, having promise of the life that now is, and of that which is to come" (I Tim. 4:8).

Regardless of which biblical passage we may be using for a text our purpose is to show that Christianity is in thoroughgoing accord with the wisest understanding of life. Sometimes we may wish to present this idea succinctly, by means of searching interrogations. If so, it is wise to raise our questions in such a way that the congregation will immediately feel that we are going to deal with the issue with candor and honesty.

I. WHY RELIGION?

Suppose we are interpreting I Timothy 4:8. "Why Religion?" is a thought-provoking subject which suggests we are planning to think with our hearers. An introduction, therefore, should immediately confirm this impression. One direct approach would be quickly to raise the question plainly, Why religion, anyway? Is there any real reason for it? Is it, indeed, a necessity or merely a mental and spiritual luxury? Or is it something we have outgrown?

112

These interrogations are in order, since each of us must answer them. They are, moreover, now being asked by people everywhere. So we ask the congregation frankly to face the question with us: Why believe in religion?

If there is no satisfactory explanation for believing in Someone above us, Someone greater and wiser than are we, it will doubtless mean ultimate capitulation to secularism and materialism. It could result in our moving closer to, and possibly uniting with, the atheistic religion which is sweeping over Asia and seriously affecting our Western world.

1. FEAR AND RELIGION

Since this blueprint is to deal with life logically, it may be advantageous to suggest certain explanations for religion which do not justify its continuance. In this section of the sermon we could briefly pinpoint some of the popular criticisms of religion. For instance, numbers of writers have insisted that fear is the explanation of belief in God. This is the basic reason for the origin of the great religions of the world, according to Lewis Browne in his widely read book, *This Believing World*.[1] Others have insisted that superstition is the seed of the tree of religion. Ignorance caused fear and superstition. Because men did not understand many things, they were afraid. Thinking that the manifestations of nature were deities, or that these represented gods, they worshiped the sun, the moon, the stars.

Now, in this modern age we have knowledge. We are in possession of facts. The light of truth has dispelled the darkness of ignorance, and science has disclosed a multitude of facts. There is no occasion for the former superstition. "Why, therefore, religion now?" many impatiently ask.

Some who are more careful with their language simply say that religion deals with the unknown. Accepting this, however, as the sphere of religion, since the unknown is so rapidly becoming known, why religion *now?* The question

---

[1]Macmillan, New York.

seems to be entirely in order when we remember that research has answered numerous inquiries and solved many of our problems. Devoted scholars have certainly disclosed unnumbered facts and are constantly on the quest for more. With this in mind, some people say that there is a need for religion until our scientific knowledge is complete. Religion deals with the unknown; there are many facts yet undiscovered. Awaiting the revelation and discovery of truth not yet revealed, we need religion.

Certainly, to some extent religion does deal with the unknown. There is, furthermore, apparently sufficient justification for religion so long as we have an undiscovered country of the mind; so long as there are numerous facts which we cannot yet interpret or explain. This reason, moreover, would seem to guarantee religion a fairly long life, for we have picked up only a few handfuls of information on the vast shore of time and space.

On second thought, though, limiting religion to the unknown only could mean its ultimate death. For the life of any religion whose future is contingent on ignorance is probably timed. Its existence could be only temporary. There can be no reason for it as soon as science has focused sufficient light on all knowledge. Sooner or later the need for religion would be sure to pass. Its death knell would be sounded. In the meantime, intelligent students would lose regard for it. Its death, though not yet in sight, would be certain.

Pursuing this line of study, using the simplest language possible and holding the attention of the congregation with every intelligent appeal to their imagination, we could then proceed to point out that there is a deeper need for religion than simply assisting us to be adjusted to unknown facts. There is something much more vital than a happy adjustment to the mysterious. To be sure, there seems to be mystery everywhere. But religion does far more than help us cultivate faith with which to meet situations and conditions which perplex us.

The greatness of the universe apparently demands mental and emotional adjustments. It awes us. When we realize that our world is only a speck of dust in what seems to be boundless space, we begin to grope for something that can hold us steady. Lost, confused, and afraid, we seek guidance. Religion at its best proposes to show us the way. It tells us how we may find the right direction. It has promise of the life that now is. Many of us, to be sure, feel like the psalmist, only far more strongly: "When I consider the work of thy fingers, the moon and the stars which thou hast ordained, what is man that thou art mindful of him?" Searching for some encouragement that will help us believe in the dignity of man, we turn to religion.

Even so, the day may come when we can take the vastness of the universe in stride. At least space travel is no longer out of reason. Granted that sometime we shall not be awed by the greatness of the universe, that some day we shall know all facts, is there still something that makes great religion vital, necessary, inescapable? Is there, indeed, any justification for it which seems to be timeless?

2. INTERPRETATION OF FACTS

Because we want to play fair with our hearers, the approach just indicated is advantageous, and at the same time, prepares them for another main section of the sermon. For in this division we can indicate reasons that take us beyond the area of discoveries. This is particularly relevant, when we remember that some say we are now launching out on our last great endeavor to conquer the universe. Here we point out that, no matter how many facts we have, *some interpretation of them is necessary.* However encyclopedic our knowledge, we always have to ask what things mean.

Science may give all the facts there are, but they still need interpreting. What does our total world situation mean? There are so many thousands of heavenly bodies the mind of man cannot grasp the number. They are so far away we measure the distance in light years. This seems quite enough to awe us; yet, we can measure the distances and weigh the planets. We have marked ability to gain possession of every type of knowledge. But much more is needed. What does it all mean? For what purpose is our knowledge? Here is matter, material substance, atoms, electrons. What is their message? Here are millions of stars. What is their purpose? Is that which we can see with our physical eyes the sum and substance of life? When we have finished measuring and weighing, do we understand everything we need to know?

This is where Christianity becomes searchingly significant. Christ says the world has meaning, man has worth, and there is One who will guarantee the fulfillment of his divine plans. He affirms the faith of one who sang his creed long before Jesus was born: "The heavens declare the glory of God; and the firmament showeth his handiwork" (Ps. 19:1). So Christ asserts that there is meaning in the world. He insists that what we see and touch speaks of Something greater than itself.

Here we have night and day, joy and sorrow, peace and pain, life and death. What does it all mean? We know something of human existence, just as we know much of what is in our material world. But what is the meaning and message of all this? Eventually we must know what life itself says. Religion insists that there is a message! Christianity declares: "There is Spirit, a divine Personality. There is God above man, and man is more than a body. These great ideas give significance to life. They make meaningful every possible experience."

This is the message of religion. It says there is purpose for us, and that life, therefore, need not be futile for any person. Human existence means something. Each of us can discover a divine plan. Religion takes us by the hand and leads us to the top of the mountain, from the summit of which we can see life whole. We see things in their proper relationships. We observe harmony in the world. This leads

116

us to an understanding of God and of our own spiritual natures which makes it possible to see "things" as Christ saw them. Only religion at its highest can give us this perspective.

When "the things which are shaken" seem to include everything we have treasured; when the revolutionary forces of our world apparently have no regard for our past security or our present hope; then we become painfully aware that we need help. We may not find strength, but without it we live in despair. We know confidence is necessary if we are to face life boldly.

Superficial optimism is obviously impossible for intelligent people. Pessimism offers us nothing to "go on." Courage could hold us together and keep us going. This is what God offers.

3. Peace of Mind and Heart

When we have made this justification for religion quite plain, we are on the highway of logic that leads to life. But it is still necessary to point out that facts and their interpretation are not enough. We have hearts as well as minds. We want more than knowledge and insight into its meaning. That is why, as ministers, we can say there is much more. Christianity which, for many of us, is religion at its best, is the only philosophy which makes life completely reasonable. Christianity does not deny reason. Rather, it is harmonious with our best thinking. Indeed, Christ makes it possible for us to understand life. Without the great spiritual interpretations which Jesus has given us, we are continually baffled by the experiences we face. It is the Master who puts together the puzzle of human existence.

He brings us God who reaches down into hearts and souls to satisfy our deepest longings. He brings peace and comfort, quiet and rest. He soothes tired feelings and banishes restless thoughts. Whatever we may say about the process, those who have experienced these blessings eagerly testify that God does remove guilt and sin and in its place gives peace and power.

4. POWER FOR LIFE

We are not made for Nirvana. "Life is real, and life is earnest," we remind our hearers. No matter what other resources we may have discovered, without the strength to overcome the forces which oppose us, we are frustrated. This fact presents us with the opportunity of underscoring the need of understanding and receiving a power greater than ourselves.

So we again raise the vital question: Why religion? And we give the answer: *Life must be lived on the plane of spiritual satisfaction.* After we have an interpretation of facts which meets our deepest desires, and that peace of heart that steadies our nerves, we want a sense of conquest. We want to triumph. Christ makes that possible. He is the victor over all circumstances and all conditions. He gives us spiritual power; through him we overcome.

By His hand we are led aright through life. Thousands still sing:

He leadeth me, O blessed thought!

Those who know the reality of religion find new meaning in the words: "The Lord is my shepherd; I shall not want. . . . He restoreth my soul: he leadeth me in the paths of righteousness for his name's sake. Yea, though I walk through the valley of the shadow of death, I will fear no evil" (Ps. 23:1-4). So Paul writes: "Now unto him who is able to do exceeding abundantly above all that we ask or think. . . ." And the author of Hebrews declares: "He is able to save . . . to the uttermost" (Heb. 7:25).

Stanley, the intrepid explorer, underscores the truth of these affirmations. "Lost in the African jungle, constrained at the darkest hour to confess myself helpless without God's help," he wrote, "I vowed a vow in the forests wild that I would confess His aid before men. I besought Him to give me back my people. Nine hours later we were exulting with a rapturous joy. I am utterly unable to attribute our salvation to any other cause than a gracious Providence." Testimony like this emphasizes a real reason for religion. For this is not the word of a religious specialist or of a fanatic. It comes from a sophisticated man of the world. Whether or not we should assert that Providence will act in this particular way—often it does not—we can learn how to put ourselves in the care of One whose wisdom and strength are adequate for every human need.

It is, of course, necessary for the speaker to raise no false hopes. He should show that different individuals handle difficulties in various ways. Certainly most of us do not win the same fortunate results that Stanley enjoyed. Nevertheless, God gives us inner resources for the severe trials and onslaughts of life itself. Thus we can pinpoint this truth: Conditions and situations which seem to defeat us are themselves indications of the inevitable need of resources greater than ours. That such resources are available is the promise of Christianity. It offers us the possibility of triumph. Even when we are defeated without, there can be victory within. So we say religion is essential just because there are situations for which power greater than our own is necessary. With Christ we can triumph. We can learn so to face life that we can say of it:

> It were a well-spent journey
> Though seven deaths lay between.

Christianity brings such quality and worth to those who accept it that we are sure that life is not merely worth living; it is a joyous experience. This is the testimony of those who know Christ personally.

Frequently we must sing a song of life in the midst of death. We need the gift of joy most when sorrow encompasses us. Where there is weakness, we must be strong and bring comfort. Christ makes that possible.

Consider this woman, a member of Dr. R. J. Campbell's congregation in London. She vividly demonstrated the

119

possibility. She earned her bread by singing. Once when her child was critically ill, she fled the stage after her number, running from the theater while loud applause demanded an encore. Arriving home, she learned that her child was worse—indeed that there was no hope for her. When the little girl asked for a song, the mother, who was too choked up to respond to her audience with an encore, took her child in her arms, paced the floor, and sang:

I think when I read that sweet story of old,
  When Jesus was here among men,
How He called little children as lambs to His fold,
  I should like to have been with Him then.

Here is a mother facing what they must who live long enough to deal with death. Yet she meets the crisis with a song—a hymn of love and confident faith. She was like the intimate friends of Jesus, who have had something in the present to assure them of a future which, instead of being dreaded, is anticipated with joy.

We come to a conclusion for this sermon which underscores the reasonableness of religion. The pattern we use will vary, since the congregation and the immediate circumstances are determining factors. One of the easiest is that of a summary. In this we can insist that an interpretation of the universe which sees in it a spiritual meaning, pointing to a life of present triumph and to a future of blessedness, offers an adequate reason for religion.

"Why religion?" we ask. And the answer comes ringing back: Because life and death have meaning and worth for us only as we know the God of Christ who gives us a quality of life that is eternal.

· II. Proof That Persuades

Another way of using the same sermon blueprint is vividly suggested by the text, "Come and see" (John 1:46). The same words are used in John 4:29, and offer additional material or an alternate biblical background. In a brief in-

120

troduction for this message we could say that here is a passage as fresh as the new day, as streamlined as modern
life, as up-to-date as tomorrow. Its very spirit is in harmony
with our scientific age. It is like saying: "There is no need
to discuss this matter. It is foolish to waste time arguing
about it. Come on down to the laboratory. We will take a
look at the tests to see what they show. Let's examine the
facts. We will see for ourselves."

This, we indicate, is the spirit of both life and religion
on their highest level. Certainly it represents the attitude
and character of Christianity. Although popular opinion
often associates dogmatism with religion, that viewpoint is
far from the idea of Jesus.

A natural procedure from this introduction would be to
summarize what happened in the incident as we find it in
the Fourth Gospel. This widely accepted technique, used
by ministers of a past generation, offers many advantages.
One of these makes possible the use of the Bible story in
a way to suggest expository preaching. At the same time,
we can so present the few relevant verses that we prepare
our hearers for the emphasis on the importance of reason.

Thus we call the attention of the congregation to a fas-
cinating and intriguing story. The Samaritan woman was
thrilled and excited. Her conversation with Jesus was so
entirely different from any she had ever imagined that she
forgot everything except this strange person. Convinced
that he was the Christ, she could not reprove the people
to whom she breathlessly told her story. She could not
blame them for doubting. Her story *was* incredulous. But
she did insist that in fairness these friends ought to go see
for themselves.

Certainly she had justified her right to speak so earnestly
to her friends. She had left her pot of water and had run
back to the village to announce the thrilling news. We of
the Western world can scarcely hope to understand the full
import of her action. Maybe we would more nearly grasp
the meaning if we were to think of our leaving bags filled

with money, forgetting how valuable our possessions were and running off, obsessed with a startling news story or a great discovery. Water was so scarce that it was like gold. There were not too many wells in the little country, known later as Palestine. Consequently, it was inevitable that there should be many pitched battles over the sources of supply. Life depended on water. This fact, cut deeply in the lines of the mind, was a part of the subconscious. No one forgot it. Yet this woman was so deeply moved by her conversation with Jesus that she forgot for what she had come.

In this way we prepare for the major emphasis of the message. Always we need to get to our central theme as quickly as possible—without leaving any suggestion that we are pressed for time.

It is easy to indicate quite plainly that what this woman said is precisely what the church says when it is thoroughly Christian. This is always our invitation, "Come and see." All sincere devotees of Christ are constantly saying the same thing. It is the fairest, the most reasonable invitation ever extended.

Another possible approach is to use the element of surprise, that is, of the unexpected. We could point out that it is not the men of faith but the doubters who have been the dogmatists. Actually the finest religious people are not dogmatists. The doubters are the cocksure people who are so certain of their views that they can laugh at the testimony of religion. This attitude of brushing off truth with a smile has prevailed so long that it masters most minds today. The dogmatism of doubt is still pronounced, very widespread and deep-seated.

But doubt is negative. It keeps us from accomplishing anything of great worth. Doubt never built a Brooklyn Bridge. Doubt never dug a Holland Tunnel. Doubt never rode in the cab of a steam engine across America or flew in the cockpit of a plane across the Atlantic.

Therefore, we insist that Christianity is at least reasonable in its approach; it asks that we examine the evidence for ourselves before we make up our minds. "Come and see," it invites. We impress our hearers with the obvious truth that it is unfair to deny without examining the evidence. Christians have seen and experienced the power of God. The homiletical material used in this section of the sermon will, of course, depend on the members of the congregation. But history amply shows that rich and poor, scholars and uneducated people, youth and age, business and professional men—individuals from all areas of life—invite us to make the scientific test, follow the light we see, give Christ a chance to use us, commit ourselves to the Christian way. This material may well include references to certain individuals we know intimately, and possibly, a personal word of testimony. Thus, we, too, can say:

> *What we have seen and felt*
> *With confidence we tell,*
> *And publish to the sons of men*
> *The signs infallible.*

This is the assurance of reason which springs from personal experience. It is at the center of many sermons that arrest the attention and hold the interest of doubters who seek the truth.

X

A PLACE FOR PROPAGANDA

Some ministers shrink from using the term "propaganda" in the same sentence with the word "gospel." The gospel is good news, they remind us, not propaganda. It is fact, not fiction. It is truth which can be tested, not argument offered for the purpose of convincing minds. To speak of a sermon of propaganda suggests a lack of spiritual delicacy such as should characterize every Christian minister.

Although at times this criticism seems valid, it discloses a failure to understand the term used, since there is good propaganda as well as bad. There are affirmations of thrilling and exciting truth, as well as declarations which produce doubt. The Christian sermon of propaganda has as its purpose that of stating and reiterating the truths which Jesus emphasized, in such effective ways that they become lodged in the minds of our hearers and eventually win their devotion.

Of course, we must be exceedingly careful about any statement which we make with insistent confidence. As students of the New Testament, we realize how important it is to understand what Jesus said. We are eager to proclaim his words with the accuracy and the earnestness which characterized the first-century Christians. Here is purposeful proclamation of truth which pursues us relentlessly, as it does those to whom we preach.

If the term "propaganda" describes this kind of preaching, there is surely no occasion for an apology. The Communists are not afraid of this word or of the techniques which make their program effective. They indulge in propaganda day and night. They know what they want, and they have confidence in their methods of securing it. Writing in the *Red Star*, Professor Togerow, of Russia, says, "The relics of religious faith must be wiped out by systematic propaganda."[1]

As the first major atheistic religion, communism challenges Christianity every step of the way. The disciples of Marx and Lenin portray a fervor which, strangely enough, reminds us of the enthusiasm and dedication of the early Christians. For they also have a philosophy, a program, and a passion. Churchmen who are afraid of zeal will hardly be able to compete with the Communists. For the same reason such churchmen will not appreciate the marked earnestness of the minister who discusses a New Testament truth which makes heavy demands on loyalty to God and service to his cause.

I. WHY GO TO CHURCH?

Consider, for instance, this subject: "Why Go to Church?" Understanding the importance of the services of worship, many ministers use this emphasis as a means of cultivating devotion to the total program of the church. Whatever may be the primary motive, proper attention to church attendance certainly is in order.

A text which suggests basic principles of loyalty to, and love for, the program of worship is Luke 4:16: "And he came to Nazareth, where he had been brought up: and, as his custom was, he went into the synagogue on the sabbath day." This, moreover, is a text which has "found" us, not one for which we searched.

An introduction that is both biblical and historical is in order. We could easily begin, therefore, by pointing out that Jesus did not have to make up his mind to attend religious services. He habitually did so. His parents had directed him wisely and lovingly during his childhood and youth. They had helped him to cultivate fine attitudes of devotion. With obvious naturalness, he had come to love

---

[1]Quoted by C. A. Coulson in *Science and Christian Belief* (Fontana Books, London), p. 17.

the Law and the synagogue. The spirit of devotion which these had provoked colored all his thinking.

Many people today, to be sure, do not consider church attendance relevant to their own religious responsibilities. Insisting that life is not what it was when Jesus lived, they tell us that the Christian church does not make the same appeal to them that the synagogue did to Jesus. Thousands have broken early habits of church attendance. Others have never formed them.

1. FAMILIAR REASONS FOR CHURCH ATTENDANCE

With this in mind, in the first main division of the sermon we may enumerate familiar and popular reasons for church attendance. There are large numbers to whom the church still makes an appeal. For them it has drawing power. It provokes sincere sentiment. It arouses warm emotion.

Some of us are attracted by the beauty of many church buildings. The architectural lines, the stones set together with careful design, the towers that point skyward, the open doors—all these beckon to us with a happy welcome.

Congregational singing appeals to many of us. Some who are not familiar with the language of music, who actually understand very little of its delicate harmonies are, nevertheless, noticeably affected by the singing of great religious hymns. We are deeply moved by words like these:

> O worship the King, all-glorious above,
> O gratefully sing His power and His love;
> Our Shield and Defender, the Ancient of Days,
> Pavilioned in splendor, and girded with praise.

So, too, there are individuals who go to church because other people are present. Most of us are glad to be with friends. A crowd "lifts" us. "No greater torment could there be to me than to be alone in Paradise," exclaimed Goethe. We understand what he meant.

126

Religious fellowship gives a sense of security. The presence of other worshipers cultivates a spirit of kinship. Throngs of reverent devotees help us. The experience of being with them imparts power.

So, too, our awareness of spiritual needs helps us to worship with others. As we listen to stately words of devotion and ageless prayers, we soon find our own petitions silently rising from our heavy hearts. The presence of others reverently praying near us gives our meditation new force.

The words of the Bible, as they are read to us, do not simply arrest our attention; they bring encouragement to our minds. The testimonies of the prophets and psalmists speak to us with dignity and wisdom. "God is our refuge and our strength, a very present help in trouble." Something steadies us. Or our attention is arrested by Jesus' words: "Blessed are the poor in spirit: for theirs is the kingdom of heaven. . . . Blessed are they which do hunger and thirst after righteousness: for they shall be filled." These affirmations help us to discover the Power, not ourselves, that makes for righteousness.

To hear the reverent reaffirmation of great truth is also a major reason why many individuals go to church. If the gospel message is clothed in language that is fresh and virile, it can deepen our desires for goodness. New aspirations to live better come to us. No longer are we satisfied with ordinary achievements.

The church is still a bulwark for many of us. It touches our emotions. It captures the affections of our hearts. It helps us sense reality. In a day when revolutions are sweeping old foundations from under us, we are offered in the church the things which remain unshaken.

2. Habits of Worship

Dealing with reasons for attending the services of the church, we will surely indicate the impelling power of habits well formed. Psychologists insist that patterns of behavior can be set, even in young children. Some are most desirable and quite essential to good living.

As brief as the record is concerning Jesus' life, we are informed that his parents took him in his early years to the services of public worship. Thus in later life, he went regularly to the synagogue "according to his custom" to participate in worship.

It is well to indicate that our need of the church is very pronounced because of our human limitations. Regular attendance upon the services of worship can mean the difference between defeat and victorious living. When crises descend upon us we can be already inwardly fortified, as we are also upheld by Christian friends who understand and even enter vicariously into our suffering. True religious habits of worship, then, bring us human support; what is more vital, they lead us to that help which "cometh from the Lord who made heaven and earth."

Sincere worship binds our hearts and minds to our fellows who bow with us in prayer and join with us in praise. Of far greater significance is the fact that those who worship together intelligently are bound as one to God, as they are lifted to higher spiritual understanding.

A woman of the slums, while worshiping with George Matheson's congregation, came to know the gospel's power. She had long lived in a cellar, taking for granted the limitations involved. One day she astonished her neighbors by moving from her basement to a new lodging in a sunny garret. When her acquaintances plied her with questions, quite simply she answered, "Ye canna' hear George Matheson preach, and live in a cellar."

Indeed, we remind our hearers, we cannot participate intelligently and regularly in the services of worship in our church and remain on a low spiritual level. What happens to the worshiper is of supreme importance—not what formally or ritualistically occurs in the sanctuary.

Not only are we affected individually; we come to experience genuine and wholehearted devotion in trying to assist others. This brings us to learn that here we do not essentially *get*, but we *give*. We find that Christianity seeks the good, not of one only, but of *all*.

In the alchemy of this fellowship we and our people no longer suffer from the oppression of loneliness. Rather we discover the one satisfactory way to escape it. We enter into some fine fellowship with those who love us, as together we seek regularly and consciously to come into the presence of God, our Father.

3. The Family of the Church

When our parishioners understand this, it is easy to lead them logically to take another step. In the corporate worship offered by the church we do not think of each other as individuals only, but rather as members of the family of God. There are reasons for worship which have to do with benefits for the entire religious community. Any social group or nation which attempts to minimize or prohibit worship is planning its own collapse. The very elements of greatness possible for any group are determined by the reality of unseen, spiritual values. If we miss these, we miss God. A generation that does not worship does not know what to seek. Familiar with the price of many things, such people do not know the value of anything.

4. Spiritual Reality

As our parishioners worship together, however, in the spirit of the family of God, they can become aware of the presence of God. No longer need fear overcome them, for they are increasingly confident that the Being who controls the stars and guides the planets in their courses is our Friend and Father.

Thus we can show how Christian worship lifts us far above narrowness and littleness. Worshiping the God whom Christ portrayed imparts the grace of fellowship, along with the consciousness of divine dignity. It is increasingly clear, moreover, that this experience of uniting mankind into one family is the hope of our world. We could well read daily one appeal of Paul to his friends in Ephesus: "I beg you to live lives worthy of your high calling. . . . You all belong to one Body, of which there is one Spirit, just as you all experienced one calling to one hope" (Eph. 4:1-4, Phillips).

At the same time that we discuss the vitality and relevance of the church, we are compelled to confess our human failures, lapses, and sins. We have permitted other organizations to pioneer in racial fairness and social justice. At times we have talked as if changing the machinery and structure of the church means denying God. Indeed, millions of church people have been more concerned with the status quo, place, power, and prestige than they have in the character and purpose of Christ.

II. LEAVING FOR NOWHERE

Another possible sermon of propaganda is suggested by the text, "Lord, to whom shall we go? thou hast the words of eternal life" (John 6:68). We can present the issue sharply by asking: To whom, or to what, will we go if we leave Christ? Simon and the other disciples could have turned back to Judaism. So can we. But with what result? Moses is at the heart of the Jewish religion—Moses and the Law. Both are inadequate.

Law cannot save us now. The law depicts what is wrong. What we need most, however, is not a consciousness of wrong, but *deliverance from wrong*. This is what our fathers called *grace*. Thus, the very incompleteness of Judaism pointed to the need of fulfillment. If we turn to Moses, he sends us back to Christ.

1. DEAD-END STREETS

Emphasizing the truth that when men leave Christ, they do not go in any direction which promises hope, we may proceed to spell out what this means. In a very practical way we can suggest in what directions it is possible now to turn, mentally and theologically. Atheism is one of these detours. But what does this road offer? In atheism man is the highest possible being, for there is no God. Yuri Gagarin had no God to thank for his successful flight around the world.

At our highest, because we are human, we demand something beyond and above us. The higher we climb spiritually, moreover, the more keenly we feel the need of something still greater. Atheism says there is no such being over man.

We can refer to August Comte who did not say that his teachings were atheistic, but whose philosophy left no place for God over and above humanity. He tried to find satisfaction by suggesting humanity as the *Grand Etre*. But this substitute was not adequate.

So we recall Voltaire's declaration that "if there were not a Deity, we would have to invent one." Some are seeing more clearly than ever before that any nation without God has lost its real values.

Thus, quite logically, we raise the searching inescapable question: To whom will we go if we turn away from Christ? No matter how good he is, one is less than the best if he is not Christlike. If there is no God, then there is no ruler, no leader, no being in charge of the universe, whom we can worship with the deepest possible satisfaction.

Of course, agnosticism is a possibility. And in one sense, this detour may suggest a reverent and humble attitude. For most people, of course, it is not. They boast of what they do not know. At its worst agnosticism is dogmatic, declaring we do not know and cannot know what we need most to know. Obviously there is no constructive help in dogmatic doubt!

Among the possibilities of choice, we also have materialism. It, however, offers only final despair, since it says all is of the earth, earthy. It asserts that there is no soul, no mind. We can quote the words of a keen thinker of the Hebrew race who tried it, and then wrote: "Vanity of vanities; all is vanity. What profit hath a man of all his labor which he taketh under the sun? One generation passeth away, and another . . . cometh. . . . The eye is not satisfied with seeing, nor the ear filled with hearing. I have seen all the works which are done under the sun; and, behold, all is vanity and vexation of spirit" (Eccles. 1:2-4, 8, 14). Obviously here is no bouyant outlook for the future! If this writer is sure of his facts, it may be well to follow his suggestion and "curse the day of birth." At long last we have to say, "Earth to earth; dust to dust; ashes to ashes." This is the message of materialism. Byron tried it and then declared, "Life sparkles only at the brain." Afterward he wrote:

> *My days are in the yellow leaf;*
> *The flowers and fruits of love are gone.*
> *The worm, the canker, and the grief*
> *Are mine alone![2]*

In all this discussion about the inadequacy of materialism it is of the greatest importance that we never suggest a lack of concern for physical needs. The failure to see that communism *does something for the economically oppressed now* has made many churchmen blind to the reason for the appeal of that "strange religion" to the suppressed masses of the world. As one of the fathers of socialism, Henri de Saint-Simon, though critical of the Communist Manifesto, insisted that the proper concern of an enlightened church is a public works program.[3] Certainly Edward Rogers speaks with penetrating insight when he writes that if we take our gospel sufficiently seriously, we will pray for its social aspects to be "directed and energized by the Holy Spirit." The gospel "is the alternative to every plan to restore society without God."[4] Man does, indeed, need food, shelter and clothing, but these can never become a substitute for God.

If we turn from Christ, another possibility is science, once the accepted messiah and savior of many scholars, who

---

[2] "Remorse" in *Masterpieces of Religious Verse*, p. 275.
[3] See his *Nouveau Christianisme.*
[4] See *A Christian Commentary on Communism* (Wyvern Books, 1959).

eagerly worshiped at her shrine. Some are still fascinated by the knowledge which has "changed the conditions of man's life . . . (and) . . . the way men think of themselves and of the world." Sir Richard Gregory, for many years editor of *Nature,* wrote the beginning of his epitaph as follows:

> *My grandfather preached the gospel of Christ,*
> *My father preached the gospel of Socialism,*
> *I preach the gospel of Science.*[5]

Most physicists and chemists, however, have learned we cannot rewrite the Twenty-third Psalm in this way:

Science is my shepherd; I shall not want.
It maketh me to lie down in green pastures;
It leadeth me beside still waters.
It restoreth my soul;
It leadeth me in the paths of righteousness for its name's sake.
Yea, though I walk through the valley of the shadow of death,
I will fear no evil; for science is with me;
Its rod and its staff, they comfort me.

It is more than thought-provoking to note that the knowledge of our possible destruction by means of forces we have discovered has compelled many brilliant scientists to turn to religion. They know far better than most churchmen how desperate our situation is. Many would join Dr. C. A. Coulson when he insists that "science is essentially a religious activity, playing its part in the unfolding of the nature and purpose of God." Whether we agree with F. H. Bradley that "we seem to touch and have communion with what is beyond the visible world,"[6] in our best moments we know we need something above and beyond science.

Of course, if we turn from Christ, we could accept pantheism. But how would that aid us in our present plight?

[5]Coulson, *op. cit.,* p. 18.
[6]*Ibid.,* p. 141.

Pantheism says God is all and all is God. There can be no personal Deity, no Being of intimate fellowship. We want Someone who can personally justify and fulfill our eager hopes. "As the hart panteth after the water brooks, so panteth my soul after thee, O God" (Ps. 42:1).

2. CHRIST: OUR HOPE

No wonder that after living with Jesus, Simon Peter exclaimed: "Thou art the Christ. If we turn from thee, to whom shall we go?" The answer is obvious. For Christ was the portrayal of the God, who alone can satisfy our highest longings and our deepest needs.

We are ready, therefore, to discuss what accepting Christ means. Since he is the inescapable Christ we must do something with him. He met Matthew at the seat of customs. The tax collector arose and followed him. He passed by and called to some fishermen. They felt impelled to leave their nets and follow him. Jesus faced Herod, Caiaphas, and Pilate. They also had to face *him*. So do we. When we think we are free from all the persuasive influences of religion, he quietly waits for our decision.

3. CHRIST IS THE WAY

Because the possibilities suggested in the first major part of the sermon are clearly unsatisfactory and because Christ is one with whom we must deal, we are ready to indicate why he is our hope.

Consider, then, who this Christ is. Only so can we face him fairly. His character and his influence in history portray him as the authority in the field of religion and life. Suppose we were standing one day in the presence of Michelangelo, looking at a beautiful marble figure. With his keen discerning eye and superior artistic understanding Michelangelo is pointing out certain flaws in the work. He says, "Yes, in some ways it is a fine figure. But the size of the head is out of proportion to the torso. One of the hands is a bit cramped." You turn and ask a friend, "How does he know?"

Your friend answers, "Know? Surely if anybody knows, it is Michelangelo. If he doesn't know, who does? As a sculptor, he is a master."

So it is with Jesus—only in a more pronounced way. He was a master of life. He understood the value of people everywhere. He hated no person—only systems and situations that oppress persons. He loved all, regardless of their place in society or their attitude toward him.

Jesus never gave a little answer to a big question. One day when a man asked him, "Who is my neighbor?" the reply of the Master opened long vistas of meaning. No one could ever be in doubt again. He plainly said that anyone who needs us is our neighbor. Whenever anyone asked Jesus a question, or whenever he faced some problem of life, he never met it carelessly. He dealt with the great issues in a way that still challenges us.

4. Christ Leads Us

Since this is a sermon that presents a positive declaration of some essentials of Christian faith, we make it unmistakably plain that Christ is the only one to whom we dare turn. We insist he alone is the one to whom we can go. And it is now more imperative that we face this fact than ever before.

Simon is right, eternally right! Here is one who answers the heart cry of man. Why? "Because," he says, "God is like me. You see God when you see me." He gives us a personal God, one to whom we can go and find true blessedness and complete response to the deepest needs of our lives.

Thus we begin to see that the sermon of propaganda presents dogma without being dogmatic and truth without being intolerant. We are considerate of our hearers even though we refuse to compromise the challenging message of Christ.

XI

PREACHING ON UNPOPULAR TRUTH

Every time we preach a sermon that has any content of abiding worth we are dealing with unpopular truth as far as some of our hearers are concerned. This is subtly suggested by a cartoon showing the president of a woman's club as she was introducing the guest speaker. With painful incisiveness the cartoonist had this presiding officer say, "This is Professor Smith who is going to address us on 'Europe Today', and she promises to leave out all the nasty things."

Any person who speaks on Europe, Asia, or America today and "leaves out" the regrettable and disagreeable will not give an accurate picture. He will not be telling the whole story.

Popular truth is that which people happily accept and upon which they are willing to act. That means any statement may be unpopular as far as some individuals are concerned! Normally, however, when we use the phrase "unpopular truth," we are referring to that which the majority of those present have not been willing to accept, or upon which they refuse to act.

I. THE PERENNIAL PROBLEM

Obviously, there is basically nothing new about preaching unpopular truth. The prophets always faced the problem. What made them prophets was their willingness to face it and then to do something about it.

Consider Amos who cried, "The Lord God hath spoken, who can but prophesy?" (Amos 3:8). Micah exclaimed, "What doth the Lord require of thee, but to do justly, and to love mercy, and to walk humbly with thy God?" (Micah 6:8). The forerunner of Christ, John the Baptist, succeeded in getting his head chopped off because he proclaimed un-popular truth. He never would have faced trouble if he had been willing to adjust his message to the moral and ethical standards of those in places of power.

Refusal to compromise compelled Jesus to climb the hill of Golgotha. He came into a world that had lost its nerve. He demonstrated the daring of one who incarnated courage and interpreted its meaning. He depicted its necessity for us if we are to gain the strength we desperately need.

Those who accepted the challenge of Christ followed in this same way of clear-eyed faith and fearless devotion to the highest truth they knew. John Knox, constantly in trouble with the queen of Scotland, is only one among many daring proclaimers of high standards. He is a dynamic example of the basic truth that the *Christian minister does not preach sermons to be enjoyed.* The earnest preacher well understands that one of the most uncomplimentary statements a worshiper can make relative to a sermon dealing with ethics and morals is to say, "I enjoyed your sermon." He deeply appreciates what made Nehru exclaim, "We talk of our ancient culture; it is folly to talk about culture, or even to talk about God, while human beings starve and rot and die."[1]

The problems posed by selfishness, lust for power, and arrogance are always with us. But they have been multiplied and intensified by conditions so terrific that it is difficult to measure their force. It is easy to say that two philosophies of life are waging a battle that concerns the whole world. This is true, but it is an oversimplification of the truth. Good is arrayed against evil, as always. But only the naïve would claim that all the good is on the side of organized religion and all the evil is represented by the powers opposed to the church, even in Russia. We know too well how a church which allied itself with governmental leaders unconcerned for the oppressed masses made

---

[1] Quoted by Alexander Campbell in *The Heart of India* (Knoff, 1958), p. 59.

it easier for men to overthrow that government and inevitable that they should violently oppose religion. The church which they knew had forgotten the commandment, "Thou shalt love thy neighbor" (Mark 12:31).

Of course, to speak truth daringly is not pleasant when so many people refuse either to face facts or to do anything about them after they have recognized them. But we do well to remember the warning of Lord Morley: "He who begins life by stifling his convictions is in a fair way to ending it with no convictions to stifle."

Ponder the deeper meaning of the words of one of the clerics in Hugh Walpole's *The Inquisitor:* "Either this whole thing, the spiritual life, is nonsense or it's real. . . . If it's real, don't you suppose Someone is angry somewhere?" Certainly Christian ministers must love the world enough to point out its mistakes, condemn its sins, and challenge it to righteousness.

Is there, then, no means for Christian ministers to avoid controversial questions? Not if we intend to follow in the train of Amos, Jeremiah, John the Baptist, or Jesus. As most of us know, we will at least occasionally "lock horns" with powers of evil. Nor is ministerial silence on issues such as alcoholism and industrial oppression—by whatever group—a sign of wise discretion. Silence, as we have often been warned, seems to mean we favor the status quo. Clergymen who do not speak clearly on vital issues lead the masses to assume that religion invokes divine blessings upon "the powers that be."

No wonder Dorothy Sayers cuts us to the quick when she insists that neither Herod nor Caiaphas, neither Pilate nor Judas "ever contrived to fasten upon Jesus Christ the reproach of insipidity." This "final indignity was left for pious hands to inflict." We are beginning to see, moreover, that making "this story" something "that could neither startle, nor shock, nor terrify, nor excite, nor inspire a living soul" is "to crucify the Son of God afresh and put him to an open shame."

II. Principles of Procedure

Of course any principles of procedure necessitate careful study and wise training. There are directions that can save us from many regrettable mistakes.

Certainly we are aware that knowledge of history is itself a requisite. Consider eighteenth-century England when the religious life of the country took a downward trend until dismal darkness fell upon the churches. Dr. R. H. Tawney reminds us that except for a few people, considered eccentric, the idea of the church as an independent moral authority, "whose standards may be in sharp antithesis to social conventions,"[2] was abandoned. Jonathan Trelawny, Bishop of Winchester, who died in 1721, suggests the popular attitude when "he excused himself for his much swearing, by saying he swore as a baronet and not as a bishop."

"The English clergy were the idlest and most lifeless in the world," says J. R. Green, in his *Short History of the English People*. Sermons consisted largely of essays which frequently dealt with nonreligious subjects. After visiting all the London churches, Blackstone remarked that he "heard not one discourse which had more Christianity in it than the writings of Cicero." There seems to be no question that clergymen in seventeenth- and eighteenth-century England were conspicuous for gambling and drunkenness.

The issue now is whether we are so intoxicated with our own ecclesiastical programs that we have no time to study the desperate state of the world, no time to understand the "enemies" of the church, and no concern for those who do not support our own religious groups. We are impatient with those converts in the Far East—our friends—who insist that frequently Christian churches have tried to "buy" influence. We have attempted even to impose our own architecture and patterns of worship on those who wanted to follow Christ but with their indigenous forms of worship. When we say these people are too sensitive, we unashamedly con-

---

[2]*Religion and the Rise of Capitalism*, pp. 188-189.

fess that we do not have the patient charity of which Paul spoke in First Corinthians 13.

Any failure to be properly equipped with facts and skills emphasizes the importance of our having a broad historical view before we talk glibly about any situation. It means that we must make careful study of the past and the present. Only so do we gain understanding.

All this emphasizes the necessity of frankly asking ourselves what are the moral and ethical conditions to which we need to give our attention. If there is an ethical standard, what is it? Certainly any truth we preach must be valid before we present it. It must be truth in the present, for tomorrow, the day after, and for all the days to come. Only so is it dependable.

We must deal, therefore, with fundamental principles rather than with immediate symptoms. These principles necessarily include (1) treating every person as an end in himself instead of a means to an end; (2) accepting as any basic principle for life only that which we are willing for every other person in the world to make his own.

III. METHODS OF UNDERSCORING TRUTH

Although the problem of preaching on unpopular truth is a perennial one, this does not mean we can use the methods employed by our predecessors. Jonathan Edwards forces us to face this fact. In the eighteenth century, he cried: "The God which holds you over the pit of hell, much as one holds a spider, or some loathsome insect over fire, abhors you, and is dreadfully provoked: his wrath towards you burns like fire: he looks upon you as worthy of nothing else but to be cast into the fire."

Many people now smile when they read this statement, but the words were once searching and powerful. Today we have to find the power of which Edwards' sentences are only symbols, if we are to convince minds and convert hearts. Our language will be quite different, but arresting attention and holding interest is still a requisite of any preacher.

Whatever the terms we use or the methods we employ, the message must always be true. This means we must distinguish between prejudices and moral principles. This is not easy, but it is essential for every procedure.

The scientific attitude is one with which we can never dispense. It requires us to exercise care not to speak when we are under undue emotional strain, and never to use one of our momentary whims as though we were dealing with a fundamental principle at the center of Christianity. Calm, confident insistence is essential.

Recall a meeting in Albert Hall in behalf of the League of Nations at which Earl Grey presided. In a brief address he set forth the reasons for an attempt to organize the spiritual forces of mankind. Lord Robert Cecil gave the chief speech. He said: "If we are to have peace, we must first obtain recognition for the fact that the good of mankind as a whole does actually exist." At first there was no heckling, but later when, with emphasis, he added that the League must at last include all nations, there was an uproar.

"Must Germany be allowed to enter the League?" he was asked.

"*All* nations," the speaker repeated.

"Traitor! Traitor!" the shout arose.

Confusion reigned. One who was present tells us that Cecil was as cool as one of the snow-capped peaks of the Alps. He calmly wiped his glasses. The proceedings went on.

The same spirit of calm and deep regard for all mankind must possess us as we deal with other people, places, and conditions. We must be so sure of our truth that we shall have the confidence knowledge and Christian conviction always produce.

IV. The Christian Motive

Remembering the Christian prophets of the first and second centuries A.D., we will constantly recall our essential problem and seek to be guided by the central motive as we deal with any unpopular truth.

First of all, there is a need. This is the real reason we deal with unpopular truth. Of course, we could be adroit and meticulously careful. We could try to evade or avoid issues that are "controversial, disturbing, and inevitably provocative of trouble." Obviously, there are numerous subjects of importance that may be presented without creating antagonism and dissension. Why not emphasize only these? Why deal with the Sermon on the Mount during war? Or why, during days of racial tension, stress Peter's vision when he was told to eat what was before him and not to call unclean that which God considered clean? Certainly we want to be liked! We insist that we must win friends if we are to influence people. But we are compelled to recall that there are two kinds of popularity—the ephemeral and the permanent. More frequently than we may realize, we must sacrifice the one for the other.

Just because courage is so important, we must watch against overemphasizing it. A constant concern for our motives will help. Otherwise we may find ourselves denouncing some individual in order to win the support of a group who enjoy seeing others persecuted. Paradoxically enough, this may earn for us a certain kind of support and partial popularity, even though our message is really unpopular. But such a reason for preaching is a long sea mile from the Christian motive, and it is especially dangerous in times of revolution.

A wise consideration of the attitude Jesus constantly demonstrated will save us from unreasonable denunciation. It will also help us cultivate Christian methods of procedure. What is appropriately called "friendly reasonableness" is much more effective than most fiery attacks. Frequently it is better to "whittle down our big stick and use it for a baton."

Our problem goes even further than convicting or convincing. We are to convert to good—not commit to evil.

Some contemporary preaching seems to leave the hearer with the feeling that the sooner he goes to hell the better it will be for everybody. This is not Christian preaching. It may be giving vent to one's pet peeves or expressing bitter anger, but it is not the winsome appeal of Christ.

We must not merely seek to please God more than men; we are to consider the eternal welfare of those we serve rather than their momentary pleasure.

Recall Lafcadio Hearn's story of an Oriental hero who owned and worked a highly valued rice field on a hilltop from which one could overlook the sea. During an earthquake one day, from his high vantage point the owner of the field watched the ocean as it swiftly withdrew from the shore. It suggested a terrible, destructive leap. That leap, of course, would become a tidal wave. Down below were this man's neighbors working their fields. Realizing their danger, this farmer did not hesitate a moment. He set fire to his own cherished rice ricks. Then he ran to the temple bell. Hearing the bell, his neighbors rushed to help him, only to discover that he had deliberately started the blaze. As they bitterly denounced him, saying he had jeopardized the possessions of the entire community, the farmer smiled and pointed to the sea. Seeing the swirl of waters over the fields they had just forsaken, suddenly his neighbors realized the cost of their salvation. They looked upon a man who had sacrificed his living and risked the wrath of his fellows in order to save them.

It may be wise to contrast the spirit of the hero of Hearn's story with the willingness of many people to remain silent in a day of danger. The sea of sane human relationships does seem to be withdrawing from its accustomed shores in a "menacing crouch." As a friend insists, when we give no word of warning lest we lose our popularity and prized possessions not merely are we responsible for the losses others sustain; but we are responsible to God.

Ultimately, indeed, each of us must choose between certain "fortunate" moral adjudgments and the eternal standards of our religion. The Christian prophet has insight that makes him realize Christ's principles will outlast the passions of men and that the man who proclaims them in season and out "may suffer sinister consequences, as did his Master." Nevertheless, such men are confident that in the long run Christ and his cause will win.

Across the long years the motive of expedience is not justified. "Blessed are ye, when men shall revile you, and persecute you, and shall say all manner of evil against you falsely, for my sake. Rejoice, and be exceeding glad: for great is your reward in heaven: for so persecuted they the prophets that were before you" (Matt. 5:11-12). Remembering this, we may be wise enough to become scientific students of truth rather than "smooth divines" in the pulpit.

Each of us may well learn certain lines of Timothy Dwight's famous poem written before he accepted ordination. As has been suggested, some of the words are quite disturbing.

> *There smiled the Smooth Divine, unused to wound*
> *The Sinner's heart with hell's alarming sound.*
> *No terrors on his gentle tongue attend;*
> *No grating truths the nicest ear offend.*
> *He bowed, talked politics, learned manners mild,*
> *Most meekly questioned, and most smoothly smiled;*
> *At rich men's jests laughed loud, their stories praised,*
> *Their Wives' new patterns gazed, and gazed and gazed;*
> *Yet from their churches saw his brethren driven,*
> *Who thundered truth and spoke the voice of heaven.*
> *"Let fools," he cried, "slave on, while prudent I*
> *Snug in my nest shall live and snug shall die."*

V. THE SPIRIT OF THE PROPHET

This discussion of our responsibility leads immediately to a consideration of the spirit in which our message is to be delivered. Manifestly we are never to permit ourselves to be trapped into uncontrolled anger by those who oppose us. Rather we are to see their failures as an indication of great need to which we are to respond in the spirit of Christ. For this reason we are always to speak our message in Christian charity. This self-control is especially vital during crises which are phases of a world revolution—contemporary conditions that most of us manifestly will continue to face for a long time.

At our best, we know that we must always demonstrate in our lives what we express verbally. Readers of *Alice in Wonderland* will agree that "the best way to explain it would be to do it." As Gladstone reminded us, "One example is worth a thousand arguments."

This truth is vividly illustrated by the attitude of P. Carnegie Simpson who had picked up malaria, possibly on a trip to Palestine. The malady had brought him near death's door when he called in a brilliant young physician, a personal friend. The doctor, though he was "destroying both his practice and himself by intemperance," pulled himself together, attended Dr. Simpson faithfully, and in the end almost literally saved the minister's life.

Immediately thereafter, the physician lapsed into his old habit and died. Dr. Simpson was so moved by the doctor's devotion that later, in writing his autobiography, he expressed hope for his young friend at the Great Judgment. Whatever we may think of the theology involved, Dr. Simpson's attitude challenges us to test all our messages by the Cross.

One of the apocryphal stories concerning Jesus, which deeply moves all Christians, etches this truth on our minds. It depicts the Master outside the heavenly city apparently waiting for someone. Some of his disciples reprove him for not joining in the joy of the hour. "Why do you remain out here?" one bluntly asks. "I'm waiting," replied Jesus, speaking slowly; "I am waiting for Judas."

Such, then, must be the spirit of the Christian preacher when he delivers any unpopular message.

XII

THE SERMON THAT SHOCKS

The sermon that shocks is not new. All the prophets of the Old Testament were familiar with its purpose and character. Indeed, the crises during which they lived helped to make them what they were and gave them much of their message. Recall some of their arresting sentences:

Woe unto them that join house to house, that lay field to field, till there be no place, that they may be placed alone in the midst of the earth! (Isa. 5:8).

Woe unto them that seek deep to hide their counsel from the Lord, and their works are in the dark, and they say, Who seeth us? and who knoweth us? (Isa. 29:15).

You only have I known of all the families of the earth: therefore I will punish you for all your iniquities (Amos 3:2).

And I will turn your feasts into mourning, and all your songs into lamentation; and I will bring up sackcloth upon all loins, and baldness upon every head; and I will make it as the mourning of an only son, and the end thereof as a bitter day (Amos 8:10).

Woe to her that is filthy and polluted, to the oppressing city! (Zeph. 3:1).

Students of the New Testament readily recall John the Baptist's searching and disturbing proclamations. Who has not felt the impact of his dramatic denunciation and of his startling warning?

But when he saw many of the Pharisees and Sadducees come to his baptism, he said unto them, O generation of vipers, who hath warned you to flee from the wrath to come? Bring forth therefore fruits meet for repentance: and think not to say within yourselves, We have Abraham to our father: for I say unto you, that God is able of these stones to raise up

146

children unto Abraham. And now also the axe is laid unto the root of the trees: therefore every tree which bringeth not forth good fruit is hewn down, and cast into the fire (Matt. 3:7-10).

With peculiar and penetrating power, Jesus also used words that shocked his hearers. Unfortunately many people are so superficial in their thoughts concerning religion that they tend to forget or ignore the many illustrations of Christ's incisive and cutting language. He was the Master in this area of presenting truth. It was one of the methods he used to fulfill the purposes of the prophets and impress his hearers with the seriousness of conditions. Consider how relevant some of his words are to contemporary conditions:

Woe unto you, scribes and Pharisees, hypocrites! for ye compass sea and land to make one proselyte, and when he is made, ye make him twofold more the child of hell than yourselves (Matt. 23:15).

Woe unto you, scribes and Pharisees, hypocrites! for ye are like unto whited sepulchres, which indeed appear beautiful outward, but are within full of dead men's bones, and of all uncleanness (Matt. 23:27).

Woe unto you, scribes and Pharisees, hypocrites! because ye build the tombs of the prophets, and garnish the sepulchres of the righteous (Matt. 23:29).

If any man come to me, and hate not his father, and mother, and wife, and children, and brethren, and sisters, yea, and his own life also, he cannot be my disciple (Luke 14:26).

Ye serpents, ye generation of vipers, how can ye escape the damnation of hell? (Matt. 23:33).

The Son of man goeth as it is written of him: but woe unto that man by whom the Son of man is betrayed! it had been good for that man if he had not been born (Matt. 26:24).

Recall, too, how the early Christian writers employed this same technique:

Woe unto them! for they have gone in the way of Cain, and ran greedily after the error of Balaam for reward (Jude 11).

Go to now, ye rich men, weep and howl for your miseries that shall come upon you. Your riches are corrupted, and your garments are motheaten. Your gold and silver is cankered; and the rust of them shall be a witness against you, and shall eat your flesh as it were fire. Ye have heaped treasure together for the last days (Jas. 5:1-3).

The second woe is past; and, behold, the third woe cometh quickly (Rev. 11:14).

And I beheld, and heard an angel flying through the midst of heaven, saying with loud voice, Woe, Woe, Woe, to the inhabiters of the earth by reason of the other voices of the trumpet of the three angels, which are yet to sound! (Rev. 8:13).

Whenever we conclude any serious reading of the Sermon on the Mount—the most shocking sermon ever preached—we are driven to meditate on its effect on Christ's hearers. It is written, "The people were astounded at his teachings" (Matt. 7:29, NEB).

Verbal shock is a technique of the modern psychiatrist, but it has been used for centuries. It is not simply a means of gaining attention. Rightly used, frequently it can help bring calm out of storm, sanity out of insanity, peace out of turmoil.

Obviously each minister must decide how well equipped he is to use this pattern of presenting any truth. In every instance, however, the very nature of this method requires delicate care as well as prayerful preparation. In the chapter dealing with unpopular truth, I have discussed a few of the essentials for any approach which startles one's hearers, since so much prophetic preaching follows this procedure. Manifestly when any of us attempt it, we should *plan, prepare,* and *speak with great care.*

The text that "finds us" gives us our message. For the sentences in the Bible that speak to us can speak through us. Ponder the candor of Christ: "In the world ye shall have tribulation" (John 16:33). To go with this text, "Let's Face the Music!" is a simple topic which suggests that the speaker is going to explain what Jesus says. In a world alarmed by the threat of nuclear warfare and frightened by hydrogen bombs, this kind of preaching becomes almost too easy.

Suitable for an evening service in some churches, "Don't Fool Yourself!" is a theme with meanings much deeper than the slang suggests. Still another procedure is suggested by the text: "I am alive for evermore" (Rev. 1:18), with the fitting topic: "God Is Not Dead!" Certainly any subject for this sermon should arrest serious attention without suggesting superficial sensationalism.

I. WHY I CANNOT DO AS I PLEASE

"Why I Cannot Do as I Please" is a theme which readily lends itself to the pattern of "the sermon that shocks." For a text to substantiate and forcefully present this idea, one may choose Galatians 6:7: "God is not mocked: for whatsoever a man soweth, that shall he also reap." Indeed, the preacher will find in both Old and New Testaments ample material with which to explain this topic. Many "judgment day" passages are certainly relevant, and Jesus' words in Matthew 12:36 may be used to summarize one phase of the sermon. "But I say unto you, That every idle word that men shall speak, they shall give account thereof in the day of judgment." The topic logically leads to introductory emphases similar to some indicated in the paragraphs which follow:

I cannot do as I please if I please to do anything in particular. Whenever I choose any goal, or any objective, for my life, I must follow the path that leads to this purpose. Always I deliberately limit myself because of a specific aim.

I cannot do as I please if I choose any kind of dependable character. My deeds and attitudes will be determined by the purpose I decide to pursue.

God himself cannot do as he pleases, if he remains God. Let us say it reverently: If he is the Christlike Deity of whom the

149

New Testament speaks, he will invariably be guided by that standard of divine character. To put it sharply, God cannot be both capricious and have the character which Jesus insisted he does have. Divine by nature, in attitude and deed he will always manifest a gracious spirit, a Christlike character. Browning emphasizes a vital part of this truth when he writes:

> *The loving worm within its clod*
> *Were diviner than a loveless God*
> *Amid His worlds, I will dare to say.*

With care we emphasize that God cannot do an unrighteous deed and remain divine. We point out plainly that any act that is immoral, or unmoral, runs directly athwart dependability. God must always be true to himself and consistent with his character. In the same way, and for the same reason, you and I cannot do as we please if we keep intellectual integrity and ethical honor.

1. RESPONSIBILITY FOR INFLUENCE

Somewhere in the sermon dealing with this theme, the alert preacher may well remind his hearers that vitally related to all principles which concern character is another reason why we cannot do as we please. If we consider our obligations to our fellows, the deeper meaning of this fact reaches out into every area of human existence. Because what I do affects other people, I must assume responsibility for my influence. Ethical obligation is inherently bound up with every decision I make. I have to face the moral import of my deeds.

For obvious reasons, a sermon presenting this truth requires clear-cut logic and mental integrity. Careful procedure necessitates our taking each step with reason. Since our purpose is to arrest attention and assist our hearers to turn into the path of high ethics, we are eager for them to feel the inescapable reasonableness of the message. The following paragraphs may suggest how to focus attention upon this point.

Although most of us are aware of limitations on our wills, we know that we can, to some degree, choose what we wish to do and be. Of course, heredity is a fact we cannot deny. We are the result of what has gone before. But choice is real. It is this that makes us persons. Without the power of choice, we would be animals—at best, mere individuals. Because we are persons, we are aware of ourselves, and we have the privilege of making decisions.

Heredity and environment affect any choice we make; they are factors which we are compelled to consider. But they also serve to *confirm* the power of choice, for they indicate what others have chosen and the *influence* of their decisions on us. To say that heredity and environment are potent only serves to underscore the significance of choice itself.

By using the first person singular, we may be able quickly to depict the power, purpose, and social responsibility of personal decisions.

What *I* choose has influence. Manifestly I am myself affected by what I decide to do! I can choose, I must accept obligation for this privilege.

The same principle holds with reference to my relationship to others. I swing my hand across this bit of space. Since I am out of reach of other people, nobody particularly worries. If, however, somebody's nose is in the way, that person worries. Later *I* may worry. All this, indeed, may happen in a split second, if the person whom I strike has reflexes which work quickly. Since I am responsible for what I do, I must assume accountability for the results of my deeds.

This law of moral responsibility prevails in all areas and is valid for every age. It is timeless. It is most significant during a revolution. Ours is not a Robinson Crusoe world; even that representative of individualism discovered his neighbor, Friday. We are living in a social order. What one member of society does affects his neighbors, those who live near and those who reside in more distant places. The more complex society is, the more necessary it is to take individual influence into consideration.

World War II forced us to recognize interrelatedness.

We discovered that there is one big economic family. Many of us first had our attention arrested by the rationing of gasoline and of automobile tires. Other parts of the world were part of America's social order.

Now all of us see that what happens in Moscow affects the stock market in New York. And what occurs in Southeast Asia influences decisions made in Washington. This interrelatedness will become more pronounced and increasingly clear, even to the readers of daily newspapers.

Again, we will not quickly forget parental responsibility if we prayerfully meditate upon the serious import of the truth suggested by these simple lines:

> *A father and his tiny son*
> *Crossed a rough street one stormy day.*
> *"See, Papa?" cried the little one,*
> *"I stepped in your steps all the way."*
>
> *Ah, random childish hands that deal*
> *Quick thrusts no coat of proof could stay.*
> *It touched him with the touch of steel—*
> *"I stepped in your steps all the way."*
>
> *If this man shirks his manhood's due*
> *And heeds what lying voices say,*
> *It is not one who fails, but two—*
> *"I stepped in your steps all the way."*
>
> *But they who thrust off greed and fear,*
> *Who love and watch, who toil and pray—*
> *How their hearts carol when they hear:*
> *"I stepped in your steps all the way."*[1]

Pursuant to the ever-deepening seriousness of our theme, any minister could deal with material similar to the content of these paragraphs:

---

[1]Roy Temple House.

As the result of an argument over a little roadway, a young man in western North Carolina killed one of his neighbors. During the trial, before the jury brought in a verdict of guilt, witnesses testified that the father of the young murderer had urged his son "not to take it" and "to get even." His words, repeated again and again, sank deeply into the mind of this son. The result was murder.

When the presiding judge was ready to pronounce sentence, he first took time to address the father of the confessed criminal. Stating that this parent was more guilty than his son, the judge pointed out that the law could deal only with the son; but if justice finally had its way, the father would have to expiate for the same crime.

Recognizing the self-evident fairness of this judgment, is it reasonable to think that in the court of eternal justice any individual who has made it easier for others to sin will go "scot free"? Reason and fairness obviously join to deny this possibility. In many ways the influence of some people is evil.

As a result, others suffer. In a universe controlled by integrity those who think will not evade their moral obligation. If ours is a world in which *right* will finally rule, we must ultimately deal with justice.

2. Sins of Omission

In a sermon on moral accountability it is often wise to include a discussion of our responsibility for failures which we could have avoided. One of the harshest judgments Jesus ever passed was "Inasmuch as ye did it not . . ." (Matt. 25:45). Any adequate discussion of the implications of this "verdict" would involve the gracious deeds which might have characterized our daily living, the appealing winsomeness of Christlike attitudes which we could have chosen by offering God the chance to give us the Divine spirit and communicate to others, through us, the message of love.

Such a sermon will certainly include some reference to our failures to hear and heed the words of Christ: "If any man will come after me, let him . . . take up his cross" (Matt. 16:24). Because we can choose this obligation, we necessarily have the privilege of rejecting it. Otherwise we are only a superior breed of cattle, and, as W. R. Maltby has reasoned, "The history of the Christian faith is just a chapter in mythology."[2]

This theme of accountability is not popular. Most people seem to want religion to do something for them, not to help them recognize their duty to God and society. This idea, however, makes it all the more important for us to use material which presents the subject of responsibility in sentences plain enough for all to read.

3. THE POWER OF THE POSITIVE

Before the sermon is concluded, some preachers will be eager to emphasize the privilege of positive dedication, suggested by Jesus' words: "Inasmuch as ye have done it . . ." (Matt. 25:40). Here again we can show that crises bring opportunities. Discussing the tremendous difference that hours spent in God's presence make in our characters, we can suggest how even our conversation may be dedicated to speaking for Christ, and how our lives may become meaningful by small as well as great services graciously rendered as unto him.

If the sermon is evangelistic, one may refer to what occurred one evening when Charles G. Finney was preaching in Rochester, New York. Many lawyers came to hear the famous minister. Doubtless their interest was intensified because Finney himself had been an attorney. One night, up in the balcony, sat the Chief Justice of the Court of Appeals of the State of New York. As he listened to Finney's logic, he became convinced it was accurate. Convicted by its spiritual truth, he was compelled to face this question: "Will you go forward like an ordinary man to the anxious seat?" (The latter term was used by evangelists for the front row of seats to which individuals went who were concerned about their deep religious needs.) At first something in the heart of the Chief Justice rebelled. At last he said, "Why not? I am convinced of the truth of that man's posi-

---

[2]*The Significance of Jesus*, p. 94.

tion. I know my duty." He got up from his place in the gallery, went downstairs, and then came to the stairs back of where Finney was preaching. In the midst of his sermon, Mr. Finney felt someone pulling on his coat. When he turned, there was the Chief Justice of the Court of Appeals of New York.

The minister quietly asked, "What is it?"

The Chief Justice replied, "Mr. Finney, if you will call for people to present themselves at the anxious seat, I will come."

Mr. Finney stopped his sermon and made a call for those who were concerned about their salvation. The Chief Justice went down and took his place on the front pew. According to the account we have of the incident, almost every lawyer and barrister in the congregation followed him. The records show that most of the lawyers in Rochester made a profession of religion during this revival. It is said, moreover, that one hundred thousand people registered "decisions for Christ" in twelve months in that district.

Showing how this story interprets the Bible truth we are presenting, it would be easy to conclude the sermon with a summary statement. We can remind our hearers that every man is not a Chief Justice of Appeals. Every person does not have the same opportunities. But there is not a man, woman, or child who does not have some power of persuasion. For that personal capacity and the results of its use each individual is accountable. At the moment, however, instead of giving attention to obligation as such, we can urge our hearers to think of the high privilege of adding our influence to the eternal power of good which is in harmony with the character and life of Christ!

Of course there are congregations that will consider this incident and the techniques it suggests out of date. Obviously it would be difficult to use this reference in most university chapels. But the principle is valid! We do not want to admit that our failures, as professing Christians, have created the atmosphere in which communism has been able to thrive. Just as important is this fact: While many irresponsible people denounce Marx and Lenin, they forget there is no way to overcome their propaganda save by offering mankind something better than they have promised.

Furthermore, there is ample material we could use in any pulpit. Dr. Karl Menninger declares "that most Americans today exist without purpose and without significance. They have no articulate philosophy; they do not live within any frame of reference."[3] The head of our FBI states that crime, juvenile delinquency, and disrespect for law and order are rife. We also recall that when our missionary enterprise began in India, the people insisted that Christianity was not *true*. Later they declared that it may be true, but it is not *new*. More recently millions have pained us by pointing out that Christianity is not *you*. That is, you and I do not represent it.

II. Stop! Look! Listen!

The same pattern of preaching, dealing with different ways of arresting attention, could be presented by explaining texts such as these: "For he taught them as one having authority, and not as the scribes" (Matt. 7:29), and "Whatsoever a man soweth, that shall he also reap" (Gal. 6:7). A subject portraying the vital message of these Bible statements could be "Stop! Look! Listen!" An introduction appropriate for this theme could include these ideas:

The familiar warning, Stop! Look! Listen! is not simply a signal for our physical protection. It concerns our total welfare. It is no longer merely a popular device to keep people from being killed by cars, trucks, and trains. The very future of society depends upon our willingness to obey this injunction in every area of life.

We read signs men erect for our physical safety. But when we

[3]*Newsweek*, October 24, 1955.

become really intelligent, we also realize that we must be constantly alert for the "signals of God." They concern our present and our future welfare. Particularly is this true in these revolutionary days. God's signs are flashing vividly before us. No one need miss them.

Another possible presentation could deal with three groups of people: (1) The few who make things happen; (2) those who watch what does happen; (3) the hosts who have no idea of what has occurred.

It would be in order to insist upon our giving attention to the qualities of Christian leadership. In this way we could easily and naturally lead our hearers into a consideration of the first point, which describes part of our contemporary situation. Certainly it would be logical to point out that those who "watch what happens," but refuse to study contemporary conditions, will be of little aid to our world. When we turn deaf ears to the prayers of humanity or to the demands of those who are seriously concerned with human welfare, we are not in a position to deal helpfully with present-day difficulties.

It would also be in order to indicate how easily we can ignore unpleasant truth. The fact, indeed, that there are so many people with "indoor minds" is nothing less than tragic. Writing of Russia, shortly after the downfall of the old regime, Raymond Robbins emphasized this point by describing how the privileged classes had followed the social rounds all their "self-sufficient lives." They thought that they were adequately protected. There seemed to be no reason for refusing to indulge in frivolities of every kind.

Robbins vividly depicted how the socially elite had drawn their silken curtains across their windows. They were, therefore, unable to detect the black, ominous influences moving in the common life of Russia. Because of "indoor minds" their thoughts and imaginations never went out into those vast open spaces where a new social order was gathering momentous force. It is now easy for students of those critical years, particularly discerning readers of Dostoevski and Turgenev, to see how the revolution was gaining impetus with ever-increasing force. But can *we* see the black clouds ·about us in *our nation and our world?*

Obviously, it is necessary to refer to those voices to whose words wise men give attention. Unfortunately, there are foolish people who stop their ears because they do not like what people are saying: Determined to live indoors mentally, we may join them by refusing to give any attention whatever to the world about us. This is the preface to tragedy.

There are, indeed, raucous voices, bitter with hatred, to whose warning of imminent danger we are inclined to turn deaf ears. A few years ago Dr. Goebbels was saying: "A Jew is for me an object of physical disgust. I vomit when I see one. . . . Christ cannot possibly have been a Jew. I don't have to prove that scientifically. It is a fact. . . . I treasure an ordinary prostitute above a married Jewess."

We tried to ignore this crank and what he was saying. But Hitler joined him in putting this item of racial hatred on the agenda of every parliament in the world.

Again, we can refer to the voices of hatred which were clamoring for attention long before Hitler came to power. But we stuffed cotton in our ears and angrily pulled down the shades. Most of us refused to hear or see. To do so would have made us uncomfortable. *We were too busy forgetting God ourselves.* Besides we insisted that America was safe. Why worry?

Today when Christianity's fiercest competitor, communism, is gaining force with unbelievable rapidity, a distinguished general of the Marines declares that only one in ten young Marines could present a reasonable contrast between communism and democracy. Americans, he added, spend far too much on alcohol, tobacco, reducing aids, and narcotics.

At long last, we are beginning to realize that what happens *anywhere* can happen *anywhere else* in the world.

This is added reason for insisting that when we become lovers of truth, we will be eager to *think* and *act*.

This question, therefore, becomes inescapable: How many of us are aiding the Soviets by our sheer indifference and unconcern? This is no academic interrogation.

A book fair, held in New York a few years ago under the sponsorship of the *New York Times Magazine*, gives us a clue to the value our society places on God and his truth. Those in charge of the fair arranged what they called a library for a model home. It contained five hundred books attractively displayed. But there was no selection of books on religion. The three or four dealing with this subject were included because they were literary classics. There was not a single one in the five hundred specifically in the field of religion which had been published less than two hundred years ago.

As Halford Luccock disturbingly pointed out, this omission is all too indicative of a characteristic blind spot. It suggests not merely the state of many homes, but also the condition of millions of minds and hearts.

It is true that later some books dealing with religion were added to the list for a model library. Is our "renewed interest" in religion, however, because we are now frightened? Is it an emotional concern, seriously lacking in moral and ethical content? Is it psychological or theological?

Certainly Christianity demands that the *means* we use for cultivating character must match in integrity the *end* we desire. When we adopt techniques of terror, we create terrible and tragic conditions. Arbitrary force always produces fear. *Only God can use great power without being corrupted by it.* That is because he remains God.

So we may continue to stimulate the thinking of our hearers by reminding them that *indecision is impossible.* "It is either a planetary Pentecost or planetary destruction."

Properly presented, the sermon that shocks should point the way to complete salvation—personal, national, and world-wide.

159

XIII

GOOD NEWS

The gospel is good news. Evangelism is this good news being *proclaimed* and *lived*. The evangel is itself the heart of Christianity. To ignore this truth is to abandon our religion. To understand it is to help turn a revolution into a spiritual rebirth. If ever there were a day for making this meaningful, it is this one.

Unfortunately, we must admit that some who have claimed to be evangelists have unfairly prejudiced the thinking and warped the attitudes of many people. At times, indeed, they have made their personal interpretation of *judgment* synonymous with *good news*. The term "tragic," therefore, is not too strong to describe what has happened. This fact underscores additional reasons for our learning to think clearly with regard to evangelical religion, as we plan with care to proclaim the good news, especially at a time when most people wish they could believe in goodness.

Some ministers, to be sure, hesitatingly acknowledge a lack of enthusiasm for evangelism. A few readily confess their major concern is with "other emphases." Some of these insist they are weary of offering people what apparently they do not desire or cannot believe is dependable. Perhaps a still larger number have not dared face the problems involved. They have not studied the deeper meaning of the gospel and thus have missed its major implications.

I. Religion and Reality

It is, therefore, of supreme importance that by some means we should gain confidence that we are dealing with reality when we present the gospel. Firsthand experience is obviously essential. It leaps over the pulpit, across the empty spaces of aisles and pews, into the hearts of our hearers. This kind of genuineness strikes fire with the congregation.

A phrase used by directors of drama suggests how important this meeting of minds and hearts is. Frequently during rehearsal a good director feels the weakness of a scene and insists, "That won't play!" He means, of course, that the action or dialogue will not leap across the footlights. It will not reach the audience.

1. MAKE SERMONS "PREACH"

Likewise there are sermons that will not "preach." We may speak clearly the words we have written, but they do not say what we had hoped they would. They do not reach the minds, emotions, and wills of the people. They seem to have little relevance. Sometimes our thinking is cloudy and our lack of personal knowledge of the truth we are presenting is too obvious.

It is for us, then, to study contemporary conditions with courageous concern for human welfare. Thus we gain understanding of how and where to direct our messages. Studying our people we also learn what our best dramatists have discovered—that anyone who expects to achieve success on the stage must remember that life is on the other side of the footlights. One's performance has meaning only to the degree that it is related to the lives of the people out there. Thus with knowledge, insight, and personal experience we have something real to say. We are confident that God is and that he knows what life is all about; he knows what is going on here. He knows where he is going and has the ability to arrive and the capacity to take care of every person who gives himself unreservedly to him. In this faith we can speak to others who long to believe.

Thus if we know where life is and what it means we understand that the personal and social phases of Christianity constitute one single whole. Too many of us have failed to see that the hell in our world is a reflection of what has been in our hearts—*of the hell that is now there.* Actually, the salvation of individuals and the redemption of society cannot be separated. Politics must be Christian and states-craft must be spiritualized. These results will not follow until there are Christian leaders who can discern what is radically wrong with us and our world, and who can accept God's power for the purpose of letting him use them to make a new world. This is what makes Christian evangelism so significant for our critical and tragic day.

Good news becomes meaningful because there are bad facts—painful truth that forces us to face despair. We can correctly evalute peace because we have seen so much war. Therefore, we point out that salvation assumes sin from which to be saved. In our most discerning moments we understand why Paul exclaimed: "Who . . . can set me free from the clutches of my own sinful nature?" (Rom. 7:24, Phillips). The good news is this: There is One who can set us free. So Paul shouts exultantly: "I thank God there *is* a way out through Jesus Christ our Lord" (vs. 25).

Conversion, therefore, signifies nothing less than a personal commitment to, and faith in, Christ; second, sacramental union with "the redeemed"; third, recognition that salvation is the gift of God, not a prize we win; and fourth, a giving of self to the redemptive spirit and causes of Christ. Joost De Blank is emphasizing what many students of Christianity have said, when he points out that conversion is an act of the past, a process in the present, and a consummation in the future.[1]

With these facts in mind, we begin to learn the tremendous importance of certain basic principles for proclaiming the gospel during a revolution. First, we must preach the same truth our forefathers proclaimed, without the idea of *sameness* making it dull. Fresh approaches, new light on old truths, vivid language—all these are essential more than ever before. Second, we must preach the law of discipline, but always with a deep love of life and of people. Certainly the Old Testament can be used for evangelistic preaching, but it must always be interpreted in the light of the New.

[1]See *This Is Conversion* (Hodder and Stoughton, London).

Again, we are to use various techniques with technicolor. In our day we need not expect to gain happy results with the kind of preaching which belonged to the era of black and white movies. The message today must be interesting and so relevant to daily living that eternal truths will constantly challenge our hearers. The timely must always be set in the timeless. It is not a question of either the one or the other, as though we were compelled to choose between the two. The everlasting must be set in contemporary conditions.

Above everything, the evangelistic message must be vivid and vital. It must live, and it must be so dramatically presented that it makes people want to know the secret of life.

2. MAKE OUTLINES SIMPLE

The simplest kind of outlines are preferable for the evangelistic sermon. Consider a text often used: "Behold, I stand at the door and knock" (Rev. 3:20). Here is a possible outline:

   I. *What* God does when he enters our lives:
      1. Purifies thoughts
      2. Ennobles feelings
      3. Directs our wills
      4. Gives divine character to our deeds.

  II. *Why* we should permit God to enter:
      1. For our own sake
      2. For the sake of society
      3. For the sake of the world
      4. For His sake!

 III. *When* should God enter?
     Now!

Although outlines as plain as this are not always possible or in order, usually the simplest outline is much more effective for an evangelistic message than one which is intricately involved. For instance, the preacher may use these three words as the titles of the main divisions of a sermon dealing with the challenge of Christ. (1) Come! (2) Become! (3) Be gone! This he tells his congregation is what the essence of Christ's challenge is. He invites us, "Come unto me all ye who labor and are heavy laden" (Matt. 11:28). He assures us, however, that when we accept this invitation something happens, as he explained to Nicodemus. (See John 3:1-7.) Zacchaeus personally discovered what it meant. It is forcefully demonstrated in Matthew's life. For Christ never leaves us where we are, to enjoy comfort for its own sake. He tells us, "Be gone!" "Go ye into all the world, and preach the gospel" (Mark 16:15). The message of personal evangelism is always logical and inevitable if it is genuinely Christian. Furthermore, the effective preacher makes the text as meaningful as possible by choosing statements which point directly to the central truth of the sermon.

So, too, we use at least three types of appeal: (1) the rational, (2) the volitional, and (3) the emotional. "How much then is man better than a sheep?" (Matt. 12:12), reasoned Jesus. Again he challenged his hearers: "If any man will come after me, let him deny himself, and take up his cross, and follow me" (Matt. 16:24). Standing outside his beloved city, he cried: "O Jerusalem, Jerusalem, thou that killest the prophets, and stonest them that are sent unto thee, how often would I have gathered thy children together, even as a hen gathereth her chickens under her wings, and ye would not!" (Matt. 23:37). On the cross, he cried, "Father, forgive them; for they know not what they do" (Luke 23:34).

3. Make Conditions Favorable

If we become effective evangelists, we must gain Christlike courage, moral honesty, mental integrity, and spiritual sensitivity. Understanding the processes of others' thoughts, we will constantly cultivate reverence for God and respect for persons. For this reason we will always seek the right conditions for our message—*physical*, in the sanctuary; *men-*

164

tal, in the thinking of our hearers, and *spiritual*, as this affects attitudes which help others to catch the contagious assurance of a dedicated messenger of the good news.

Certainly as we plan our evangelistic sermons, we will keep in mind that any final decision on the part of our hearers will doubtless be preceded by a lonely struggle and a period of uncertainty. We see Paul in Arabia, pondering. There is Nicodemus, eager but troubled, as he comes to confer with Jesus at night. Irritation and opposition may often be psychological factors with which the seeker—or hearer—must deal. He will also probably seriously consider various alternatives to the decision for Christ. This is the way men think about life and what they want to do with it. Furthermore, when an individual makes a conscious, definite ethical commitment, many of the results may not be immediately observable, but if his desire for God is deep and characterized by earnestness, he will increasingly give himself to those causes for which Christ lived and died.

II. Your Greatest Hour

Specifically evangelistic sermons should portray conversion and its effects by means of texts and themes dealing with prayer, personal work, consecration, rededication, salvation, God's concern for man, and Christ as our hope. "Your Greatest Hour" is a subject which may illustrate an evangelistic pattern. Writing a suitable introduction for this sermon is not too difficult for those ministers who are familiar with the Bible or who have studied the art of cultivating mental rapport with a congregation.

Selecting a familiar text, "He came to himself" (Luke 15:17), or "Ye must be born again" (John 3:7), we could suggest that every person ought to have many great hours. We point out that it is normal to expect experiences which lift us higher than we ordinarily live and thus give us a view of things which we have not seen before. We ought ever and anon to be receiving fresh exhilarations, new mental grasps, unanticipated impulses, toward a better life. There should be hours when everything takes on a new hue. We ought to see things and people from a different viewpoint because of a changed state of mind. There are, indeed, enriching experiences which every person should happily anticipate.

However few or many there may be, most people do experience at least some high hours. The first, which has come to all of us, is the time of birth. Unconscious of it at the moment, of course, one does normally reach a day when he understands that this was a meaningful hour. Without it there could be no others. Also the day one decides his lifework casts an influence on the years that follow. Certainly the time one chooses a life companion touches with inestimable influence all other days of that person's life.

In this way it should be easy to move to a discussion of the "new birth"—the hour of which Jesus spoke so insistently.

1. WHAT IS THIS HOUR?

It is our purpose to show that there is an even more meaningful time than the day of one's birth—an occasion which is the greatest of human experiences. It is when mere existence changes to fullness of life. It is when we come clearly to see that life has eternal meaning, and then, desiring to know by experience that meaning, we eagerly give ourselves to the realization of this purpose.

The greatest hour any of us can know is when we come to believe sincerely that there is a God in control of the universe, that this God is the wisest and best Being possible, that in character he is like Christ.

Believing this, we give ourselves to that Being, receive his Spirit, and enter into the fullness of the abundant life. But this is our experience only when complete honesty of thinking directs us to receive the truth of God as we welcome his Spirit. If the day of birth is the most important one of this life, the day of new birth is the greatest of all time. It is then we learn what life really is.

We grasp this truth as we observe how Jesus dealt with Nicodemus. This "ruler of the Jews" saw life as he never had before Christ spoke to him on that eventful night. He came to realize what he had not been able to grasp before. He heard Jesus' simply spoken message, telling of the most dynamic transaction in which a man can ever have a part. So great is it, said the Master, we can call it rebirth. Our minds, hearts, souls, enter into a new experience. Our whole personality is vitally and powerfully affected. Old things have passed away; behold all things become new.

The Prodigal grasped the meaning of this experience when he "came to himself." He saw life differently. He looked upon his own condition as he never had before. He made a new resolution. He acted on his new understanding. He went home. When he came to himself, he went to his father. He was no longer a prodigal. Ever thereafter life was different with him. His experience interprets the deeper meaning of these exciting words:

> Can peach renew lost bloom,
> Or violet lost perfume,
> Or soiled snow turn white as over night?
> Man cannot compass it, yet never fear;
> The leper Naaman
> Shows what God will and can.
> God, Who worked there, is working here;
> Wherefore let hope, not gloom, betinge thy brow.
> God, Who worked then, is working now.

Recall the new life Augustine came to know. Once defeated, downcast, despairing, he came to experience a transformation so sweeping that it was obviously divine. "I opened the book and read in silence the chapter on which my eyes first fell," he writes. "I cared to read no further, nor was there need of it since at once, with the ending of the sentence the light of security was passed into my heart and all the gloom fled away." So, it is true that "the wind bloweth where it listeth," and we cannot "tell whence it cometh, and whither it goeth" (John 3:8). But *that* the wind blows no one can deny.

Some feel that the Spirit often comes in strange ways. But that the Spirit enters our lives, and with a power so great that everything is different thereafter, we can know. That the Spirit brings confidence where uncertainty has ruled is truly good news, desperately needed in a day of fear and despair.

The new birth is the most remarkable and inspiring experience that any person can ever have. It is no wonder that multitudes have sung with Philip Doddridge:

> *Now rest, my long-divided heart;*
> *Fixed on this blissful centre, rest;*
> *With ashes who would grudge to part,*
> *When called on angels' bread to feast?*

It will be important to remember that the outward circumstances surrounding any great decision or experience are secondary. This fact we can depict by means of a second major division of the sermon, since exterior conditions cannot constitute the chief factors of any inner experience.

2. WHO CAN EXPERIENCE THIS HOUR?

What happens within the heart is of chief importance. That is the reason this experience loses none of its gracious spirit and none of its matchless beauty even though we may not have fallen to the lowest moral depths, and therefore, do not have to turn our backs on a misspent life.

Horace Bushnell was aware of this truth when he wrote his daughter a letter now treasured by many students of Christian education. After this girl had entered her teens, Bushnell reminded her that she had been reared in a Christian home, that Christian influences had been purposefully thrown about her, that she had naturally walked in the path of righteousness because this way had been chosen for her. But he added that she was then making her own decisions. When she had been immature, her parents had directed her course. Now she must choose for herself. It was time that *she* decided to make Christ king, to give him, by an act of her own will, the throne of her heart.

What an hour follows such a decision! An individual chooses for himself to face toward the highest. This is the time one deliberately, happily opens mind, heart, and soul to receive the vibrant, throbbing Spirit of God. No wonder it is the greatest hour any individual can know.

In another city a young woman came forward to commit herself completely to Christ. For some eighteen years the parents of this young woman had chosen the right for her and with her. They had never been called upon to watch her wander away, abandon high ethics, or collapse morally. No one had ever accused her of being a prodigal. But as she rose from prayer, she smiled through a mist in her eyes and spoke earnestly of her personal commitment to Christ. It was the hour in which she, for herself, made Christ King, opening the door of her heart for the incoming of his dynamic life-giving Spirit.

Whatever may be the circumstances surrounding this deeply moving experience, those who thus give the allegiance of their hearts enter into a new kind of relationship. That is the reason they can heartily sing:

> High heaven, that heard the solemn vow,
> That vow renewed shall daily hear,
> Till in life's latest hour I bow,
> And bless in death a bond so dear.

The fact that the "transaction" may be calmly and quietly made robs it of none of its beauty or of its genuineness. *What happens* is of supreme importance. As Owen Brandon has pointed out—there are at least "four or five distinguishable types" with which we should be familiar.[2] To illustrate,

[2]*The Battle for the Soul: Aspects of Religious Conversion* (Hodder and Stoughton, London, 1960), p. 27 ff.

we may refer to the emotional experiences of some like Charles Finney; of the clear reasoning of others like Bushnell who was once considered an atheist, but felt logically impelled to become a Christian; of the definite decision of some like Dwight L. Moody and Phillips Brooks who gave their wills, as they offered their lives, to God. We shall be wise to explain that these differences did not alter the reality of religion in any instance.

Thus there could be a third major division of the sermon, in which we emphasize the reason for the greatness of this hour.

3. WHY IS THIS HOUR GREAT?

The only satisfactory way to answer the question, as to why the hour of decision is so great, is to observe the after life of any person who gives the devotion of his heart to Christ. It is what happens at the moment and in all the years that follow.

In his *The Everlasting Mercy,* Masefield dramatizes the story of Saul Kane. Saul Kane was a defeated, despairing man. In his desperation he cried:

> *For parson chaps are mad supposin'*
> *A chap can change the road he's chosen.*

But those who have read even a summary of Masefield's poem know that Saul Kane did experience the everlasting mercy and came to know the power which wrought a complete change in his life, turning him from defeat and despair to divine triumph. That is the experience which makes this hour great.

Like Saul Kane, some of us do have to "start over," because we have made a mess of life. Then one day we wish for the time, now apparently passed, when life was exciting and the future beckoned with bright hope. We think of our foibles and the mistakes we have made, wishing they could be corrected. But somehow the past will not come back. Then we

> *. . . wish there were some wonderful place*
> *Called the Land of Beginning again,*
> *Where all our mistakes and all our heartaches,*
> *Could be dropped like a shabby old coat, at the door,*
> *And never put on again.*[3]

A man's greatest hour—the time he actually accepts divine power—we tell our hearers, brings the answer to this prayer.

The life of fullness and richness, however, is also for those who have been fortunate enough to escape moral degeneration. The new relationship with God brings a new quality of life for every person who receives him. The divine power which we accept in this high hour is not manifested only in a new spiritual beginning. There comes also the consciousness that God is concerned for our whole life.

Another emphasis for this sermon is inevitable, since as great as this hour, or experience, may be in itself, that which makes it so meaningful is how it affects the rest of our life. It illuminates all our tomorrows with a heavenly splendor. It gives us unyielding confidence for the years that lie ahead.

Hosts of genuine Christians face the future, not merely unafraid, but eagerly, for they are sure it holds rich treasures. They are convinced of something better for tomorrow. The quality of life they know here and now convinces them that this inherent worth cannot be lost or cut off. The power they received in their high epochal hour reaches to the most crucial experience of life itself—its apparent end—and gives them strength, courage, and conquest.

When our hearers feel this and accept its dependability, although they may not even understand what blueprint the sermon follows, they know this "kind of sermon" is thrilling and exciting, because it interprets life as did Christ. The world revolution has not made evangelism obsolete but imperative, for our one hope is that we can believe in divine integrity and experience Christlike concern for all men now.

---

[3]Louisa Fletcher Tarkington, "The Land of Beginning Again."

XIV

WE DEDICATE THE COMMUNICATIVE ARTS TO CHRIST

The person who tries to do today's work with yesterday's tools will be out of employment tomorrow. This principle of life, always relevant, is especially meaningful for ministers during days of social and national upheaval. Because of the world revolution, of which all of us are a part, we dare not ignore any of the difficulties of our profession. Indeed, since the church of today faces more competition than ever before, effective techniques for communicating the gospel are of supreme importance.

Many modern skills are, of course, basically the same as those our fathers employed. What is of sweeping significance, however, is that these, too, are seriously affected by contemporary methods of mass communication. The shrinking size of the world, moreover, has made it necessary for us to study both old and new methods from viewpoints and with perspectives which could not be familiar to any former generation.

I. FUNDAMENTAL AIMS

Some principles, however, are timeless. For instance, although Aristotle's work on rhetoric was written hundreds of years ago, we can well begin any serious study of public speaking, for any purpose, with his treatise. That philosopher stated that our fundamental aim is to persuade people to accept a certain point of view, or—what is practically the same thing—to deepen their conviction with reference to an opinion which they already hold. Often, to be sure, we hope to persuade our hearers to begin a specific course of action. In any event, *persuasion is the purpose of the speaker*. This is true whether we are attempting to encour-

172

age or discourage our listeners with regard to any program or any philosophy of life. For this reason Emerson correctly says, "Speech is power. Speech is to persuade, to convert, to appeal." Obviously it always involves a speaker, a listener, and a message.

We cannot hope to master either the science or the art of mass communication without a careful study of methods relevant to modern scientific progress. One of the first skills we must learn, therefore, is how speaker, subject, and congregation can be so effectively related that Christian worship is possible, even when the speaker and his congregation are not visible to each other.

Certainly our devotion to the gospel should guide us in readily acknowledging our obligation to learn those techniques vitally related to programing and broadcasting the teachings of Christ. Mass communication, moreover, has become such an intricate part of contemporary life that an accurate evaluation of its widespread influence is not easy. The present programs of national advertising should have etched this power on our minds quite deeply.

1. GOD AND GADGETS

Nevertheless, we must keep remembering that an understanding of techniques for broadcasting and televising does not pose our most serious need. The *message* and the *messenger* are more significant than all possible means of proclaiming the Christian gospel. For basically, preaching has to do with our knowledge of and our experience of a message worthy of being communicated. *God is more important than the gadgets we use to discuss or proclaim his will.* Our heaviest responsibility, as those eager to use radio and television wisely, has to do with our rapport with God's truth as well as with his purpose and spirit. It concerns our minds, wills, and lives becoming *media* for Christ.

Thus our spiritual experiences and our means of communicating the gospel are intricately involved. Although we are confident that we are speaking eternal truth, means

173

of gaining attention and holding interest are indispensable requisites if we plan to become effective speakers.

Obviously we ourselves must be genuinely interested in our sermon. And this is even more important when we speak on radio or television than it is when we have a visible audience, for those who employ mass media have no "captive" congregation. Our hearers will remain with us only as long as they consider the subject arresting, stimulating, and thought-provoking.

These emphases are, of course, vitally relevant to every means of communication. For preaching is concerned with the man and the media, the message and the messenger, skill and salvation. "What . . . God hath joined together, let not man put asunder" (Matt. 19:6).

2. INFLUENCE OF METHODS ON THE MESSAGE

These considerations help us to evaluate correctly the influence radio and television is having or may have on the content of our message. Specifically, we must ask: What effect have modern media already had on the Christian message? Has the "cult of comfort" become too much of a substitute for the compulsion of the Cross? Also, is it true that the sermons people hear by radio and television determine the attitudes of church people more than those presented in regular services of worship?

Most students of the communicative arts believe that messages proclaimed by way of radio and television are seriously, even radically, affecting all preaching. They do not mean that sermons delivered Sunday after Sunday from our pulpits fail to challenge those who hear them. They do think, however, that radio and television messages are influencing preaching today far more than most church leaders realize or care to admit.

We need only to observe the many speakers, for instance, who want to avoid repelling or estranging their congregations, and who substitute "a truth" for "the truth." Or because they ache "for adorers," they understand quite well "the need to keep the cheering section cheering."[1] There are times when this temptation assails most of us, but contemporary conditions have made it easier to yield to it than ever before.

3. DESIRE FOR AN AUDIENCE

Eagerness for a high audience rating has, of course, become a major matter in most religious programs. We take for granted the need for hearers, but the more discerning students of the ministry realize that too much attention to numbers is dangerous. Before we are aware of our motives, which may actually become primarily an intense desire for an audience, we find ourselves presenting religion that pleases the listeners. As a result, hosts of church people will not tolerate messages that reveal God's truth and convict of sin. They want consolation, not their consciences probed with principles that Christ taught.

Consider what would happen if many speakers using mass media were to begin to address themselves earnestly to the practical applications of Christianity. These would certainly include racial democracy, high ethics in management and labor relationships, and a strong kind of Christian friendship that would destroy any spirit of unyielding sectarianism. Such allegiance to truth would prevent our putting any denominational group on a higher level than Christ, and as a result damaging the Christian program on practically every mission field.

Because, consciously or unconsciously, many who lead services of worship in our churches try to harmonize their messages with those so pleasantly received by radio and television audiences, they increase the influence of superficial theology. Certainly, far more than we often realize, church members are being conditioned psychologically by those who use mass media in the proclamation of their gospel. This becomes particularly pertinent when we observe that thousands of church members are not yet engaged in

---

[1] Roy Pearson in *The Ministry of Preaching* (Harper, 1959), pp. 14, 15.

the main business of the church, which inherently involves helping all of us live as one family in the spirit of Christ.

Should someone point out that we need to cultivate skills that will win people for the service of worship, at least part of the answer is clear. Jesus did not hesitate to drive men from the Temple when they were commercializing religion. Christianity is, moreover, not meant to be enjoyable for those who oppose its basic principles.

Actually we cannot love people as Christ did until we hate what prevents their becoming Christlike. The uniting of love and hatred has always posed a serious problem. Jesus made this seeming contradiction quite vivid in denouncing evil, yet dying for the evildoers. Now the issue has become a severe test, since there are some who seem willing to destroy those we love along with our world. Only a power greater than our own—what our forefathers called grace—will give us either the courage or the capacity to face the strain.

Planning, therefore, to study our personal and practical relationships to the communicative arts as those eager to use them for Christ, rather than for any kind of personal aggrandisement, we will examine ourselves with searching honesty. An understanding of the Old Testament prophets and of New Testament testimony is of essential importance. So, too, the Sermon on the Mount, the theology of Paul, the meaning of social redemption, the daily demands and implications of Christian salvation in every human relationship, and the requirements of the spirit of Christ are of supreme significance.

Students of the Christian message, concerned with effective techniques for presenting it, will seriously confront conditions which tend to make us ignore or contradict both the message and the character of Christ. Whatever media we employ, Christian theology is indispensable for Christian sermons. Those individuals, heard on hundreds of radio stations weekly and seen on scores of television stations, who forget that a Christian philosophy is more important than psychology and Christian character more vital than any sectarian emphasis, warn us of the subtle temptations which ministers face.

Of course, we readily admit that some speakers who ignore essential theology may do *some* good. Just as a watch which has stopped tells the correct time twice in every twenty-four hours, so even a man who is lacking in theology is almost sure to say a few good things ever and anon.

4. SELF-EXAMINATION

Instead of caustically condemning programs that are lacking in Christian content, however, it is the part of wisdom for us, who are concerned with mass media to examine our own procedures as well as ourselves. We can hope eventually to learn that it is more important to communicate to a small group the genuinely Christian message than to gain crowds and lose our souls; that is, by abandoning high ethical standards fail to cultivate Christian experience. Certainly it is much better to insist that the teachings of Christ recorded, for instance, in Matthew 25 and the truth set down by Paul in First Corinthians 13 need to be applied in every human relationship, than it is to present anything less vital even though our radio and television audience may number millions.

Paul emphasizes part of this sweeping affirmation, when he asks: "Suppose I came to you, my brothers, speaking with 'tongues,' what good could I do you, unless I could give you some . . . truth . . . about the Christian life?" (I Cor. 14:6, Phillips). And part of the truth is that we do not build the kingdom of God. He is the creator of all that is good. We can, however, give ourselves to be used by him. Keen insight, similar to this, could stab us wide awake.

Thus do we begin to see that it is not so much a lack of faith which characterizes many sermons as it is the littleness of the messages. "We've been sending faith on petty errands trying to harness its eternal claims to cure our headache or give us more poise, stripping the gospel down to a mere

Biblical barbiturate, a two-for-a-nickel sedative. . . ."[2] This smallness has been particularly true of certain radio and television messages, whose speakers seem so keenly aware of the demands for a large audience.

To find in ourselves a disposition to deal thus with the gospel should pierce us deeply. We should be reminded of how perilously near we are to that irreverence of which W. E. Sangster spoke when he described a prominent cleric at Gloucester, England. This ecclesiastical leader, strikingly attired in red and black velvet, sat on the platform during a religious service, cleaning his fingernails with a corner of the very lovely gold cross he wore suspended from a heavy watch chain. Sooner or later, we who are ministers must decide to do little more than follow the example of this clergyman, or else eagerly offer ourselves to God, so that he can use us in the redemption of his world.

II. THE COMFORT AND THE CHALLENGE OF CHRISTIANITY

It is clearly indicated, then, that we must accept the challenge, as well as the comfort, of Christianity. At the moment, our emphasis on psychological and physical help so glibly promised the individual is a glaring and disturbing illustration of our desire to *use* God, rather than *be used by him*. This lack of adequate theology, along with a failure to emphasize the gospel's social implications, makes it imperative that we understand how essential it is to know the God who is *greater* than man. Certainly the Christian Deity is better and wiser than we are, and therefore, *his* will— *not ours*—is of supreme importance.

Until we learn that "comfort ye, comfort ye" does not mean "compromise ye, compromise ye" Christ's teachings with reference to respect and concern for people of all races and nations, we are not capable of wisely using the powerful media of mass communication available today.

---

[2]Frederick Speakman, *Love Is Something You Do* (Revell, 1959), p. 46.

1. Problems Posed

All the problems posed by the present revolution as it specifically concerns mass media probe our minds and consciences even more deeply when we recall that although we are gaining in church membership, we are apparently losing the battle for morals. While we are increasing church attendance, we are not decreasing crime.

Those who sense the dangers, as well as the demands, of mass media are painfully aware of these practical issues. By their very nature, radio and television often make it easy for hearers to avoid obligations, especially those related to their own churches. Realizing that worshiping television Sunday night is not worshiping God, we can also learn that watching a religious service by means of television is, normally, not as vital an experience as worshiping with others in the sanctuary.

2. Crises Are Opportunities

A serious study of world conditions also reminds us that important methods and techniques become even more vital when we understand that crises are always opportunities. We who preach desperately need help—the aid of God himself. So do our people. We often face crises with them. If we fail them, we destroy their confidence in the gospel itself. Soon we are without a message.

The world revolution is not on the horizon or around the corner. We are in the midst of it. There must be a new, a Christian, world, or there will be no world! We must, therefore, go a step further than our national, political, and religious competitors. As we insist that we want to build a better world, we engage in the task of building it now. Only when this intent is at the center of our message, as ministers using radio and television, can we use effectively the opportunities which come with this present critical hour.

III. How to Preach

Regarding the use of descriptive material, consider the speaker who says: "Think for a minute of the condition of a starving man, and I am sure that you will give generously to this fund for the relief of war victims." Another preacher, however, expresses the same idea in a different way. He says: "See this victim of starvation—the bloated body, the shriveled arms and sticklike legs, the sunken eyes burning in their sockets, and the black lips." It is easy to agree that the latter will draw far more response than the former.

We may ask our hearers to give as generously to a worthy cause as they would pay for a ticket to the movie. This idea appeals to our feelings of unselfishness. There is, however, another procedure which is far more effective. Taking a cue from an English writer, we might say: A snowflake is about the smallest, frailest thing you ever saw. It is weaker than a feather, since it melts away. But many snowflakes block roads, isolate villages, hold up cars of food and mail, halt trains, break down houses. The little snowflake has power in it, like your dollar. By itself that dollar is not much help in meeting the needs of physically handicapped people. Put it with somebody else's dollar; add it to thousands of others. Snow these needs under with your dollars![3]

1. The Appeal to Reason

Whatever our unique emphasis, special methods, and breadth of knowledge, our messages must be vitally related to the congregation. There are certain main arteries along which we may move into the minds and hearts of our hearers, as Aristotle made clear centuries before mass media was even contemplated. Our purpose is often to prove, or disprove, some assumption or proposition with which we are dealing. This is the way of reason.

When we happily relate our skills to the gospel, the presentation of our sermon can be so clear that the congrega-

---

[3]Peter Westland, in *Teach Yourself Public Speaking* (English University Press, Ltd., London), *cf.* p. 52.

tion will feel: "This is altogether reasonable!" When the service has been concluded, and there is time for considering more objectively our message, the most logical thinkers in the congregation—seen and unseen—should be able to say to themselves: "What that man said is true!"

This method is suggested by a message entitled, "Do We Need a New God?" Robert Holmes presents the necessary emphasis with arresting sentences. With keen insight he discusses an article written to "prove" that Christianity is "petering out."

Dr. Holmes correctly insists that we do not need a new God, but new men. Pointing out that Christ insisted we "are not the only pebbles on God's beach," he writes: ". . . whether my brother turns out to be a Fiji Islander, a Russian Communist, or a man from Mars, I am prepared to concede that God is the Father of all whom He creates. . . .

"Indeed, there was a time when I could take it or leave it; but now I had better take it and live by it, not simply as a matter of courtesy, but as a matter of survival."[4] This is the urgency of our revolutionary days!

2. The Appeal to the Emotions

Another procedure is to approach our hearers by an appeal to their emotions. In one sense, to be sure, this method cannot be completely separated from any other pattern except for the purpose of considering its inherent importance.

There is, however, a distinction between the appeal to reason, for instance, and an appeal to the emotions. Suppose we are making an appeal for our hearers to help the blind. Stressing facts concerning the people afflicted by this misfortune, whether in the nation or locally, we can present various kinds of statistics, as we emphasize the duty we owe our fellow men in their distress.

From *Esquire*, June, 1959.

When, however, we become persuaders, we do much more. We know that though a statement of fact may reach intellects, we actually win the positive response of our hearers only when we deliberately plan for and seek decisions. This is especially true for unseen congregations whom we reach through mass media. Although dealing with men's emotions requires delicacy of procedure, we are less than intelligent when we fail to appeal to more than the intelligence of our hearers. Carefully studying our possible audience, we determine which emphasis we must magnify more than another, or whether there should be something of a balance between them. Always our purpose will be to aid our hearers in moving toward Christian decisions and deeds.

Manifestly, when we are truly Christian, all our sermons deal with the eternal meaning of life and the abiding value of that to which we direct the attention of our hearers. This is our privilege and responsibility, whatever our media in speaking for God.

XV

PREACHING WITH POWER

The degree to which we, who proclaim the gospel, are inspired by God measures our capacity to communicate both his truth and his Spirit to others. It indicates how eager we are to give God right of way. This is the deeper meaning of religious enthusiasm.

Inspiration is a reality for which all effective speakers and writers have been grateful. Artists, sculptors, and poets experienced it long before the Christian era. Because of an intense yearning to express their thoughts vividly and dramatically, both Homer and Virgil invoked the Muses to speak through them. Each one demonstrated that every great author is an instrument of some force, the channel of a power that flows through him.

I. INSPIRATION AND PERSPIRATION

Inspiration is not a form of magic. For us who are Christian, it is the result of deep devotion to our task. And this devotion brings moral understanding and spiritual insight. These gifts of God make it possible for us to communicate the gospel with clarity and confidence. They lift consecration to a high level. That is where it belongs in the life of every Christian minister, no matter how many different ways his dedication may be expressed. It is indispensably important when we speak to people facing crises, individuals in despair, and persons who are wondering whether they can handle the difficulties and dangers of our day. And no one can preach now without dealing with people who are troubled.

The inspired speaker is always in earnest. *Concentration,* manifested in constant study, is at the heart of all *consecration.* When we are sincere we give ourselves with a happy

183

abandon to every task that will make us channels of God's Spirit.

There are those, to be sure, who feel that it is almost irreverent to associate *perspiration* with *inspiration*. These terms, however, do not merely belong in the same company; actually they can never be separated. When we lose one, we are certain to abandon the other.

George Eliot referred to an influence which swept over her whole life as the "Not-self." She unhesitatingly confessed that she was a poor writer until she learned to permit this unseen but real power to use her.

Those who have studied the "genius" of Joel Chandler Harris will remember his telling his daughter that he was a mediocre writer until he let "the other fellow" lean over his shoulder and write for him. But "the other fellow" helped Joel Chandler Harris only when this author worked long hours, *writing like a slave*.

Recall, too, how Hugh Walpole was one day hammering away at the typewriter, when suddenly he became aware of two eyes looking at him. They were gazing from the plaster on the wall. Walpole shouted: "Go away, I am busy!" and kept plugging away. But every time he looked up, there were the same two eyes. He had to do something about them. He ripped out the page which he was typing and immediately started to write the story of those two eyes. He never would have done this unless he had been mentally receptive, eagerly welcoming the ideas that challenged him.

The Christian minister knows there is a Force above and beyond him. All his plans and purposes begin with the creative power at the center of the universe. He is aware of Another who lives *in* him and works *through* him. This knowledge, however, becomes personal only to the degree that he learns to trust God's power and give himself to the divine mind.

Thus genuine inspiration is the result of our working steadily day after day. Disciplined devotion is inescapable.

When the high moment of inspiration comes, we shall be grateful. But because communicating divine truth is our profession and a continuing responsibility, we never dare wait for what our forefathers called "divine unction." Rather we constantly train ourselves to think clearly, to read widely, to analyze contemporary conditions, and to meditate upon the teachings of Christ, as we seek to give him right of way. This concentration is indispensable in a day of doubt and frustration.

This procedure is practical as well as inspiring. By means of it, religion becomes increasingly real and appealing. Many of those who never express their hopes, because they are not a part of organized religion, feel most keenly the need for help during the revolution which now involves all areas of life.

II. POWER IN GIVING DIRECTIONS

With keen concern, therefore, we carefully study both loyal churchmen and those apparently unconcerned with religion. As we anticipate each sermon, we learn to concentrate on the needs of those to whom we are to speak. We direct our thoughts toward the central issues of their lives, keeping our messages in rapport with God's Spirit. In this way we help our hearers answer the vital and personal questions: How can we become genuinely Christian? Is a Christian life possible and practical in a day like ours?

Discipline and inspiration prepare us to proclaim the gospel with prophetic power and dramatic challenge. They make it easier to disclose the glory of the familiar.

An experience of Lorado Taft, the sculptor, is suggestive. One evening he called some friends to the porch of his summer home to see the sunset. The western sky was a fairyland of shifting shapes and colors. As the group marveled at the beauty of it, Mr. Taft spoke with such vivid language and so interestingly that his guests began to see the sunset through *his* eyes. All the while, the maid who served them refreshments was standing by unnoticed.

Suddenly she exclaimed, "Mr. Taft, may I run down the road? I want to go home for a minute."

"Bless your heart," he replied. "What do you want at home at this particular moment?"

"I want to show Mother the sunset," she explained.

"But your mother has lived here a good many years. She must have seen many sunsets."

"Oh, no," came the earnest reply. "We never saw the sunsets here until you came."[1]

And, of course, they had not!

The inspired Christian minister will make the eternal truths of the Bible come to life, and thus reveal the majesty of God and the glory of Christ, even in a day when so many deny God, and millions of others doubt that there can be a Deity.

III. Power in Delivering the Sermon

Inspiration, of course, can never be separated from the delivery of the speaker. Effective preaching, moreover, follows some personal pattern. Whatever the specific emphasis of the sermon, there are basic techniques of delivering it. When we are wise, we study all these that time will permit. Our knowledge of various methods brings added power to communicate the gospel.

1. Writing the Sermon in Full

The first choice for some ministers is to write the sermon in full and read it as it is written. This seems to exact the least nervous strain. It requires less mental burden. Although it is the desirable method for radio preaching, it is not in order for television.

Those ministers who use a manuscript effectively become as familiar as possible with their message. Some know their sermon so well they only need, at times, to glance at the typescript. There are those who frequently turn aside from

---

[1] *Courage for Today*, Preston Bradley (Bobbs-Merrill Company, Indianapolis), pp. 25-26.

the sheets and talk informally or even excitedly discuss the theme which at the moment they are presenting. Some are able to "soar" above their manuscript. They seem to make the pages "vanish" from the pulpit.

For many of us reading a manuscript regularly means a loss of power which we cannot afford. The people glance at our faces, but they seldom see our countenances. They miss the flash of our eye or the merry twinkle which interprets a sentence or dramatizes a line. It becomes difficult to provoke interest and stimulate excited thinking.

Although there is the appeal of an orderly presentation of polished phrases and rounded sentences, when most ministers read the congregation misses the fire. Often there is no persuasive power as of one pleading earnestly. Speaking for many members of a church whose minister had not learned how to read well, a parishioner wrote:

> *I do not see my preacher's eyes,*
> *However bright they shine;*
> *For when he prays, he closes his,*
> *And when he preaches, closes mine.*

When we read a weak sermon, its weakness becomes more obvious. Indeed, a poorly written sermon should never be delivered. Certainly not poorly read!

Whether we read or not contemporary conditions demand zeal and earnestness in our language, our homiletical material, and our method of delivering our message. There is no place for a preacher who is not convinced that what he is saying is truth which people desperately need.

2. Memorizing the Sermon

There are a few who still write in full and then memorize every word. The method has its advantages. If we are blessed with good memories, we know where we are going and when we will arrive. There is no paper between us and our hearers. This, of course, is a technique used by both opera and stage. Former generations were far more friendly toward it than this one.

In any event, the minister who uses this method has the advantages of writing—a necessary discipline for practically all of us. Memorizing, furthermore, saves us from the repetition of words and phrases which we use so frequently they soon become shopworn. If we have written well, we avoid redundancy. By thinking of our hearers as we write, we learn to express ideas in language they can understand.

For most of us, however, in this streamlined age, symbolized by airplanes winging their way across the sky day and night, such memorizing is not practical. We are too busy with other responsibilities. Without a photographic memory, we are not equipped for this method in the second half of the twentieth century.

The recitation method also takes some spark out of our delivery, no matter how dramatic we may try to be. Many hearers begin to feel, "Our minister is repeating word for word what he wrote last week, maybe last year, or ten years ago." And that is disastrous when events are tumbling over each other with a rush that reminds us of a torrential river, swept by a hurricane. If, however, we do memorize, we will learn "by heart" and not just "by head."

3. Using an Outline

There is also the possibility of preaching from an outline prepared in detail. We know how we will begin, and we have planned exactly how we will conclude our sermon. These parts are prepared in full, and the outline is complete enough to remind us of the substance of our sermon. Although the illustrations and poems may or may not be written in full, we can give them accurately.

Using an outline in this way has many advantages, provided we make thorough preparation for the delivery of it. We may write numerous sentences in full. We can avoid being verbose. We can memorize, or at the very least meditate on, many phrases we plan to use.

4. Extempore Preaching

Extempore preaching is also more meaningful than ever before. The difficulty is it may become literally just that—extempore! We may jot down a few words to remind us of our theme. We may write sketchily on the margin of our Bible. We may use a card which we place on the pulpit. We may not even have a card.

Some preachers, of course, can *ad lib,* and some cannot. The ones who cannot are usually the ones who attempt it. Those who can, usually know better than to try it! And, yet, at times there is a freshness and an appeal in this method which makes it possible for the mature minister to frame sentences while he is speaking. When it is not abused, this way of delivering a sermon may increase talents and personal power. It becomes of increasing force when the speaker is prepared in character, as well as familiar with many ideas relevant to the revolution of which we are a part.

5. Preparation That Becomes Power

Another possibility in presenting our message is to prepare the sermon in a detailed way, write it in full, and make every possible plan for its delivery. After reading it to ourselves ten to fifteen times—at least as many times as is necessary to have the material thoroughly in mind—we deliver it without a manuscript. Dispensing with notes, of course, requires unswerving discipline and devoted personal training. But complete preparation, followed by delivery without a manuscript, obviously appeals to most congregations.

Freedom and versatility, resilience and relaxation, belong to this style in a way we cannot acquire with any other method. Because we have tried honestly to prepare for the high hour of the religious week, because we possess necessary facts and information relevant to the Bible, literature, and contemporary life, we move steadily toward our goal.

Thus do we learn the tremendous difference between hoping we will "get by" and knowing that we have "got ready."

Mentally and spiritually prepared, we gain inner assurance, which brings power. Keen interest, expressed on the countenances of those who are coming to grips with challenging theology, is our reward when we speak with mind, heart, eyes—with our total self.

To be "free" while we preach helps us see flashes of new truth, welcome new ideas, and even form new sentences. Our sermon is fresh. The awareness that we have mastered our material and are not enslaved by it pushes back the horizons of thought and experience. We become aware that there is a new trinity: God, God's truth, and the preacher. It is a rich and holy fellowship.

This method of delivering makes it possible for us to see things in new relationships. In the white heat of a service in which we deliver divine truth direct from the flaming fire on the altar of our hearts, there come thoughts which never would have reached the mind in the study, or on the street, or even in those quiet hours of earnest meditation. This inspiration is of tremendous significance when the Communists are so sure of their message that they communicate it with zeal.

IV. PERSONAL EMPHASES VARY

All of us are vitally concerned with the process of communicating the gospel. This is our business. But we should remember that both our talents and our characteristics vary.

Every minister needs the keenest mind he can cultivate, but it must be his own mind—enriched and inspired. Individuals vary greatly, but every person who is genuinely dedicated can render some magnificent service for Christ. Preachers who have spoken with power vividly demonstrate this fact.

Consider Dean Charles R. Brown. Simple in style, human in approach, thoroughly sophisticated, always disdainful of any trickery in the name of religion, he made theology meaningful. Scorning superficiality, he made truth clear and relevant to life. Only for formal lectures did he use a manuscript. He prepared adequately and had complete command of classical, contemporary, and historical material. Undoubtedly today he would speak with clarity and conviction, when so many confused voices make for uncertainty.

Charles E. Jefferson, likewise a master in simplicity of style, had the capacity to put great truth in the plainest language. His memory made his pulpit messages dramatic. He preached with the compelling force of naturalness.

George A. Gordon made his scholarship appealing. For years he continued his work with ever-increasing influence in one of the best-known pulpits of America. He scarcely changed his physical position as he spoke, but his ideas, and earnest appeal supported by historical references and classical language, moved all in the sanctuary. It is this talent, too, the contemporary preacher must cultivate if he makes Christianity meaningful in a day when its message is being questioned, and even doubted, by millions.

S. Parkes Cadman could speak with power, because of moving ideas and a wealth of facts. A great man with a big heart, he read far more books than most preachers can examine with care. The vitality of his language is expressed in a comment he made concerning Paul. Said Cadman, on a day memorable for one young preacher, the missionary "picked up Asia in one hand, Europe in the other, and presented both continents to his Christ!"

This kind of preaching is not merely exacting; it is terrifically expensive. Martin Niemöller spoke with enough power to be thrust into prison. His uncompromising presentation of the gospel caused a "head-on" clash with the opponents of Christianity in Germany.

Dietrich Bonhoeffer was such an effective and courageous preacher that his life was taken by the Nazis. So clearly and challengingly did he dare them to be Christian that he was resented with a bitterness which reminds us of those who hated John the Baptist.

Ludwig Steil, pastor of the Evangelical community of Holsterhausen, Wanne-Eickel, died on January 17, 1945, in Dachau. His message was too powerful and exacting for the Nazis.

Bishop Otto Dibelius has boldly taken his stand against communism because he has given himself to those causes essential to Christianity. This is power.

V. The Power of the Divine

Whatever our peculiar talent, or special emphasis, there is one requisite of supreme importance. It is *God*. The Divine Spirit is our source of power.

With respect to this indispensable quality, interestingly enough, Nietzsche spoke far more wisely than he realized when he exclaimed: "These Christians must show me they are redeemed before I will believe in their Redeemer." Certainly in the confusion, resulting from revolutionary conditions, the gospel must be incarnated if it is to be vital.

Communicating the gospel, therefore, is actually possible only when we not merely have truth but when we *become* that message, so that the Divine Spirit speaks through us. James Stewart states it succinctly this way: ". . . there is ultimately only one problem of communication of the Christian message—the problem of allowing myself, yourself, as the messengers, to be taken command of by the risen Christ."[2] With reverence and in humility, we prayerfully say, "To this end was I born, and for this cause came I into the world" (John 18:37), to make real God's redemptive love.

Our message is, therefore, never a merely formal presentation of truth. That is obviously utterly impossible during the critical days of a world-wide revolution. The disciples did not say "Here is truth." They shouted, "This is the Lord!"[3] So do we every time we really preach the Christian gospel.

---

[2] *A Faith to Proclaim,* by James S. Stewart, (Hodder and Stoughton, London), p. 47.
[3] *Ibid.,* p. 47.